Why Wait?

(A Christian View of Premarital Sex)

Why Wait?

(A Christian View of Premarital Sex)

Letha Scanzoni

 A CANON PRESS BOOK

BAKER BOOK HOUSE
Grand Rapids, Michigan

PREFACE

Sex is always with us. The subject never grows old nor loses its appeal. Each generation experiences the delightful feeling that it alone has discovered this wonderful phenomenon and can appreciate it as no previous generation could. Today's young adults are no exception. In fact, they may be better informed on the subject and have fewer hang-ups than their elders. Yet, for the Christian in any generation, one crucial question must be faced: What does commitment to Jesus Christ have to do with one's sex life? Does God have anything to say about sex? In response to this question, I can say with confidence: The reading of scores of books and articles treating sex morals from various points of view, and then searching the Scriptures for guidance on this subject, has proven to be tremendously enlightening and enriching spiritually and has strengthened my conviction that God has most surely *not* left us without counsel in so crucial a matter.

This book deals with trends and questions concerning premarital sexual attitudes and behavior. Recent sociological studies indicate an increase in the percentage of women entering marriage nonvirginal so that the figure appears to be higher than Kinsey's 50 percent cited in chapter 5 (possibly as high as 70 percent). But authorities point out that there is still no sign of an abrupt upheaval, a "sexual revolution," but rather only a continuation of a trend in which the permissiveness-with-affection standard is being increasingly accepted and incorporated into courtship patterns. Some ways a Christian might want to think through these developments are discussed in this book.

Why Wait? A Christian View of Premarital Sex is designed to present an overall view of basic Scriptural principles to help persons make their own decisions. Hopefully, it fulfills the intention expressed in the subtitle by presenting a Christian perspective of sex, a perspective that has meant much in my own life and that others may find helpful as well.

Ethical guidelines for deciding about sex behavior other than sexual intercourse—for example, questions about intimate petting (how far to go), masturbation, and homosexuality—are provided in my book, *Sex Is a Parent Affair*,* which also discusses the physiology of sex.

I am especially grateful for the constant encouragement, research assistance, and insightful comments, criticisms, and advice of my husband, Dr. John Scanzoni, Professor of Sociology at Indiana University. Our many long conversations together as the book progressed, and in particular his aid in explaining the sociological aspects of marriage for chapter 7, were helpful beyond measure.

Special thanks are also due to our friend Neil Rogers, M.D., of the Indiana University Student Health Service, for taking time out from a very busy schedule to read the original manuscript. His helpful comments, suggestions, and encouragement were most beneficial. I am likewise grateful to Professor E. M. Blaiklock of the Department of Classics, University of Auckland, New Zealand, for providing valuable information in connection with my research on the meaning of the Greek word *porneia* for chapter 8.

Acknowledgement is also made to each of the publishers who have granted permission to quote from their publications, with special thanks to the editors and publishers of *Eternity* magazine for permission to use portions for this book from the article "Sex and the Single Eye," coauthored by my husband and me, which appeared in the March 1967 issue of *Eternity*.

LETHA SCANZONI

Bloomington, Indiana

*Letha Scanzoni, *Sex Is a Parent Affair*—Help for Parents in Teaching Their Children About Sex (Glendale, California: G/L Regal Books, 1973).

Introduction

"One treasure, a single eye, and a sole Master," wrote Jim Elliot in his diary at the age of twenty-one.[1] Seven years later, Jim would die with four other young missionaries in efforts to take the gospel message to the Auca Indians of Ecuador. In life and death, these men demonstrated the words of Jim Elliot's diary. Their treasure was in heaven, their gaze was firmly set on Jesus Christ, their lives were ruled by the One who demands all that we are and have (Matthew 6:19-24).

It is in this spirit that the subject of sex will be approached, because I am convinced that *only* in this way can the Christian keep this important area of life in perspective — as God intended it. Christ said, "The light of the body is the eye; if therefore thine eye be single, thy whole body shall be full of light" (Matthew 6:22, KJV). If our mind's eye is fixed on Christ alone, if there is a singleness of purpose — glorifying God in every facet of life — then we need not fear stumbling in the darkness of confusion about what to do in sexual matters. Looking unto Jesus, we shall find that "in [His] light shall we see light" (Psalm 36:9), and we can "live like men who are at home in daylight, for

---

[1]Quoted in Elisabeth Elliot, *Shadow of the Almighty* (New York: Harper & Row Publishers, 1958), p. 71. Used by permission of the publishers.

where light is, there all goodness springs up, all justice and truth" (Ephesians 5:8, 9, NEB).

At this point, you may be thinking, "Here we go again. More somber, negative Puritanism coming up! Probably more stuff on the 'new morality' being the 'old immorality' in new dress. Doesn't she know we don't 'buy' that sort of thing? Why doesn't somebody give us some real help?"

You couldn't be more wrong. I agree with you! I'm just as glad as you are to see the passing of a stuffy, hypocritical Victorianism. The open discussion of sex in our day is to be commended. There is much good to be said about the modern generation's search for *meaning* and *reasons* behind moral-ethical decisions, not to mention the current emphasis on *honesty* and the desire of young men and women to know and relate to one another as *persons* — not sex objects. And I admit that many who are condemning the "new morality" have never really examined what its proponents are setting forth. We'll be looking into these matters as the book progresses.

But for now, two matters must be stressed: (1) for whom this book is intended, and (2) its basic message. First, this book is designed for those who have opened (or are willing to open) their lives to Jesus Christ — those who accept His gift of forgiveness and the new life made possible through His death and resurrection. St. Paul said that "if any one is in Christ, he is a new creation; the old has passed away, behold, the new has come" (II Corinthians 5:17). And being a "new creation" should make a difference in one's outlook on all of life — including the matter of sex.

Thus, this book is not addressed to those who do not desire to place their lives in Christ's hands. Such individuals cannot be expected to understand and embrace the philosophy of sex outlined here. For them, there are scores of other books setting forth good and not-so-good reasons for particular moral standards. But the goal of this book is to encourage each reader to face seriously the questions: What does it really mean to live for Jesus Christ? And what does being a Christian have to do with my sex life?

Second, the central thesis of the book may be viewed as a *paradox*. It is simply this: The Christian is called to a life of unlimited freedom; but at the same time, he is called to a life of slavery. In the midst of the modern yearning for freedom from society's restrictions, or from the church's repressive rules, or from the bondage of a guilty conscience, *only the person who has surrendered to God's will is truly free!* "For freedom Christ has set us free," wrote Paul to the Galatians, and the message still holds true.

The Christian doesn't need to consider it inevitable that he be trapped in the nets of sexual enticements tossed out at him from all sides so that sex becomes his master. Nor, on the other hand, must he feel imprisoned in a dank dungeon of oppressive religious rules purported to "keep him in line." What the one who commits himself to Jesus Christ can have is a special kind of freedom — an assurance, a calmness, a confidence that banishes much of the confusion about sex matters so prevalent today. Such a person is learning, as he walks with his Lord day by day, what it is to travel a path of *true* liberty.

This isn't an "anything goes" type of freedom, however. (In fact, no such freedom exists anywhere—as even the "hippies" of the 1960s found. Every group has patterns.) "Live as free men; not however as though your freedom were there to provide a screen for wrongdoing, but as slaves in God's service" (I Peter 2:16, NEB). Free men, yet slaves! The Christian is not his own. He has been bought with a price, and he belongs to Jesus Christ. With all he is and all he has and in all he does, the Christian is to bring glory to God. "One treasure, a single eye, and a sole Master." The implications of this in formulating a Christian philosophy of sex will be explored throughout the remainder of this book.

Perhaps one further word is in order about the book's *approach* — lest any part of it be misunderstood. In each chapter, a serious attempt has been made to avoid "preachiness," scolding, or using alarmist tactics in treating the matter of sexual standards. There are no hand-wringing, gloomy predictions that the younger generation "is going to the dogs," nor are there sensational illustrations to show "how terrible matters have become." Rather, I have sincerely tried to examine the subject as much as possible in the way that contemporary college students are wondering about it — somewhat in the spirit of an earnest quest.

Many of the questions Christian young adults are asking will surprise their parents and religious leaders — perhaps even *shock* them. But finding questions startling is no excuse to dodge them. Thus, in this book, every effort has been made to be honest and to steer away from evasiveness — for without candor, frankness, forthrightness, one cannot hope to gain the ear (or the respect) of modern youth. I have attempted to understand the sex situation as it *is* (not as many people *wish* it to be) and then have tried to show that God *does* have something to say about this important area of life — and "this God — His way is perfect" (Psalm 18:30).

Because of this approach, it is suggested that the book not be scanned superficially, but that each chapter be read carefully and in order so that the reasoning is seen to unfold gradually and logically. To wrest some small part from various sections of the book, without giving attention to the total consideration of the subject, could be misleading.

Contents

Preface

Introduction

Index

1

The New Morality — What Is It?

It all started with the 1963 publication of Bishop John A. T. Robinson's controversial book, *Honest to God*. To be sure, others before him had proposed that Christian ethics could be reduced to one principle — *responsible love;* but it was this book by the Bishop of Woolwich that sparked off a new explosion in the areas of both theological dogma and morals. The fallout from that explosion drifted everywhere but seemed to settle especially on the student population.

Suddenly it seemed everyone was talking about "relativism," "situational ethics," "freedom from legalism," "the love ethic," "the new morality," "the relationship ethic," and so on. There were some who assumed mistakenly that this meant that anything goes — that now there was indeed a unique *new* morality giving license to do as one pleases without the guilt incurred by violating codes of moral absolutes. But such *antinomianism* is just as far removed from what proponents of the new morality advocate as is the *unbending legalism* they deplore.

What then is the new morality? Essentially, it is a humanist ethic which takes into account the value of *persons* instead of a blind reliance on rigid *principle* and inflexible rules. *Love* is considered the only "moral absolute" — love that cares about the needs and feelings of the other person and acts in the way thought to be most beneficial to him. Pleaders for the new morality feel that whether certain be-

havior is "right" or "wrong" depends entirely on the situation.
Moral standards, they say, cannot be "pre-packaged." We
must have a "person-centered approach" (Will my action
help or hinder my fellow human being? How can I best
show *love* in this situation?), instead of a "principle-cen-
tered approach" (e.g., the Ten Commandments). "The new
morality, situation ethics, declares that anything and everything is right or wrong, according to the situation," writes
Joseph Fletcher in *Situation Ethics.*[1]

Keep in mind, however, that not all new morality supporters are in total agreement with all of Fletcher's opinions.
John A. T. Robinson, for example, feels that "there are some
things of which one may say that it is so inconceivable that
they could ever be an expression of love — like cruelty to
children or rape — that one might say without much fear of
contradiction that they are for Christians always wrong."[2]
When one takes an overall view of the teachings of love-
ethic proponents, one sees at times wide divergence. What
they all have in common, though, is the belief that the love-
thy-neighbor-as-thyself approach provides a more mature
way of deciding one's behavior than dependence on a ready-
made code of conduct that cannot possibly deal with every
conceivable situation that may arise.

Those who set forth the new morality are thinking, of
course, in terms of all sorts of moral-ethical decisions (e.g.,
is it ever right to lie?). Sex is only *one* of the areas they
have in mind. Yet, when many people hear or speak of the
new morality, they seem to think exclusively in terms of sexual behavior. That's why one frequently hears charges that
"the new morality is *no* morality," or "the new morality is
the old *im*morality under a new label." In many cases, those

---

[1] Joseph Fletcher, *Situation Ethics* (Philadelphia: The Westminster
Press, Copyright © 1966, W. L. Jenkins), p. 124. Used by permission
of The Westminster Press and of the SCM Press Ltd., London.

[2] John A. T. Robinson, *Christian Morals Today* (Published in the
U.S.A. by The Westminster Press, 1964. Copyright © SCM Press,
Limited, 1964), p. 16. Used by permission of the Westminster Press,
Philadelphia, and the SCM Press, London.

who make such statements have never bothered to read what new morality advocates are actually saying, or possibly they have received false impressions from sensational newspaper reports. But we must be honest and fair. If evangelicals are going to evaluate a certain position, it is only courtesy (and common sense!) to first examine that position before launching a wild attack!

(Incidentally, the term "the new morality" wasn't coined by its proponents but was first used by the Supreme Sacred Congregation of the Holy Office of the Roman Catholic Church in a 1956 pronouncement *condemning* situation ethics. The Pope feared that such a "non-prescriptive" ethic could be used to justify birth control, for example; or it might be cited by an individual Catholic in defying the Church's authority or even warranting one's decision to *leave* the Church if he felt such action would bring him closer to God.)

Since this book is specifically about *the Christian and sex*, let's consider what the new morality *does* say about sex behavior.

First, the new morality questions the church's traditional teaching that "sex outside the bonds of marriage is always wrong." Situationists feel that such an unqualified statement is unrealistic — perhaps even cruel. Might there not be *some* circumstances for *certain* people at *certain* times, they ask, which could make permissible — even desirable — premarital, extra-marital, or post-marital (i.e., in the case of a person widowed or divorced) sexual relations? Does the law or the church have any right, they argue, to dictate to an adult man or woman how he or she should satisfy normal sexual needs so long as no other person is harmed? Thus, they feel, the law of love is the only way for the individual to decide what is right *for him* in the realm of sex. "Whether any form of sex (hetero, homo, or auto) is good or evil depends on whether love is fully served," writes Joseph Fletcher.[3]

---

[3]Joseph Fletcher, *op. cit.*, p. 139. Quoted by permission.

Second, the new morality is deeply interested in inter-personal relationships. Some love-ethic supporters are quick to criticize the *Playboy* philosophy which tends to treat women as *objects* instead of as *persons*. To "use" or exploit another person for gratification of one's own sexual desires is not considered fair play. It is a failure to apply the law of love and thus is to be deplored.

Third, the new morality puts much stress on *motivation* and *attitude* and is concerned more with the *why* of sexual behavior than the *what* of what does or doesn't take place in a person's sex life. This is no doubt one reason the new morality is discussed so widely among the student popula-tion. It appeals to the modern quest many are undertaking to search out *reasons* behind moral ideals. It fits in with the contemporary emphasis on absolute honesty in regard to sex as well as in other matters.

Many Christians seem to be more upset about the implica-tions of the new morality *as it applies to sex* than they are about its application to any other area. One reason for this may be that traditionally among Christians, sexual sin has tended to be regarded as somehow worse than any other type of sin. This notion, though prevalent, is by no means Biblical. Fornication, adultery, and homosexual acts are lumped together in the New Testament right alongside such sins against God as envy, strife, gossip, deceit, boasting, disobedience to parents, anger, dissension, jealousy, slander, foul talk, and the like (e.g., Mark 7:21; Romans 1; Colossians 3; Galatians 5). Spokesmen for the new morality are cor-rect in decrying the church's smug hypocrisy in condemning sexual transgressions while shutting its eyes to many of the other areas mentioned above and all the harm they cause. Alert Christians have, of course, pointed this out long be-fore the current discussions on morality. The late C. S. Lewis summed up the matter succinctly when he wrote that "a cold, self-righteous prig" who never misses church may be much closer to hell than a prostitute — even though, of course, (Mr. Lewis adds) it's better to be in neither category.[4] The fact is that there are historical, social, and cultural reasons which lie behind the church's contention that sexual transgressions are the worst kind of transgressions. We'll examine some of these reasons in subsequent chapters.

One beneficial effect of the widespread discussion about situation ethics is that it might force many Christians to re-examine and really think through their own views on sex. True, some may feel that this is a bothersome and unnecessary effort — that it's far easier to hurl epithets at the new morality supporters. But others may find they have actually learned something by giving consideration, for example, to the warnings against exploiting other persons and the importance of looking not on overt behavior alone, but on motivation and meaning as well.

However, another reason Christians are disturbed about the new sex morality is that some of its proponents have used illustrations that strike many as being rather extreme and perhaps more sensational that illuminating. For example, a theologian said that the healing and redemptive love of Christ was present when a woman, in the English film, *The Mark*, went to bed with a man who had been sexually attracted to little girls and by her action delivered him from his obsession, giving him confidence in his ability to have normal adult sexual relationships. The prostitute in the Greek movie, *Never on Sunday*, is praised by some for helping a moralistic young sailor erase his self-doubts and gain a sense of meaning and identity when she arranges matters so that he admits his sexual desires and finds he is capable of successful sex functioning.

Some new morality pleaders ask why a woman with no prospects of marriage should be denied the experience of giving birth to a child of her own, whether by natural means or through artificial insemination, if she so desires. Fletcher suggests that there might be occasions where an

---

[4]C. S. Lewis, *Mere Christianity* (New York: The Macmillan Co., 1952), in the chapter entitled "Sexual Morality."

unmarried couple might, "if they make the decision Christianly," decide to have sexual intercourse for some specific purpose, such as forcing a selfish parent (via the girl's pregnancy) to consent to their marriage.[5]

One of the most talked about illustrations of the book *Situation Ethics* is the avowed story of a German mother interned in a Soviet prison camp in the Ukraine during World War II, who found that the only way she could be released and returned to her husband and children would be if she were discovered to be pregnant. After carefully thinking it over, the woman asked a friendly guard to impregnate her; and when her condition was verified, she was sent back to Berlin. Her family was overjoyed, despite her admission of how she had arranged her freedom; and the child born of this extra-marital union was loved intensely because it was because of him that the family was reunited. Joseph Fletcher calls this "sacrificial adultery" and asks whether this mother might not have done "a good and right thing" in such a case.[6]

It is not our purpose to comment on these particular illustrations nor on other hypothetical situations where one might face unusually difficult moral decisions in the realm of sex. Rather, these examples are cited only to give some idea of what certain situationists have in mind when they state that no code can satisfactorily deal with all circumstances.

The new moralists insist they are not arguing for promiscuity or any other form of *irresponsible* sexual behavior — although, of course, they are often accused of this. This is because the term "new morality" is indiscriminately applied to all sorts of positions, including that of the extremists who argue for total sexual freedom with no restraints whatsoever. John A. T. Robinson, for example, realizes that because of his approach to the question of sex before marriage he has been charged with "advocating laxity and immorality." But,

[5]Joseph Fletcher, *op. cit.*, p. 104.
[6]Joseph Fletcher, *op. cit.*, pp. 164-165. Used by permission.

he insists, his emphasis on taking into account "the primacy of persons and personal relationships" as the starting point in deciding whether or not to participate in premarital sexual intercourse "is to plead for a much more searching and demanding criterion of ethical judgment, both inside and outside marriage, than the simple application of an external rule. The ground on which the decision must be based is what deep Christian love for the other person as a whole person (as opposed to exploitation and enjoyment, even if mutual) really demands — and that within the total social context."[7] (Incidentally, some of his statements that immediately follow these remarks sound almost like a plea for conventional morality, i.e., the inadvisability of premarital sex relations.)

Again, we must keep in mind *what* the new moralists are really saying, and we must remember that there is variance even among the main spokesmen for this viewpoint. We must be honest if we are to answer their arguments intelligently.

For the committed Christian who sincerely wants to obey Christ, however, the new morality lacks an added and essential dimension. This is because, with all its emphasis on the worth of persons (which is certainly to be commended), the new morality somehow seems to crowd *God* out of the picture. It simply doesn't go far enough. "You shall love your neighbor as yourself" is the *second* great commandment. To love *God* with our entire being — heart, soul, strength, and mind must take first place (Matthew 22:36-40). It is on these two commandments *taken together* that "depend all the law and the prophets," said Jesus.

Some proponents of the new morality parry this by saying that we love God *through our neighbor* — that God never calls for any love to be directed exclusively to Himself, but is only interested in our love for our fellow-man. Of course, it is true that a genuine love for God will prove itself in its love for others (see I John 4:19-21), but this doesn't rule

---

[7] John A. T. Robinson, *op. cit.*, p. 42. Quoted by permission.

out the fact that in addition God *does* want us to direct toward Him our devotion, our worship, our adoration, our
affection — in short, our *love* (Deuteronomy 6:5; 7:9; 10:12;
11:22; Matthew 4:10; Joshua 22:5) — a love so great that no
other love should be permitted to equal it (Matthew 10:
37-39; Luke 14:26, 27). And Jesus Christ said, "If you *love*
me, you will *keep my commandments*" (John 14:15). He
spoke of His own obedience to the Father and used this as
an example for *our* obedience. "If you keep my commandments, you will abide in my love, just as I have kept my
Father's commandments and abide in his love" (John 15:10).

Furthermore, Christ specifically stated that He did not
come to abolish the law and the prophets, but to fulfill
them. Never did He speak lightly of the Ten Commandments. In fact, He warned against relaxing them in the
least (Matthew 5:19). By showing that we are guilty of
disobedience and sin by our *inner attitudes* just as much as
by overt acts, Jesus actually gave even greater force to the
commandments. In only one case, that of the Sabbath commandment, does Jesus' stress on motives and attitudes seem
to liberalize a command. All of the others take on a more
binding nature than ever before when seen in this light.

The problem is that most people have been taught to
think of the Ten Commandments as distant, harsh, cold
absolutes. But from Matthew 22:37, we see they are really
intended as principles for the maintenance of a love relationship with God. To fulfill them is to love God. Not to
fulfill them is to declare allegiance to another god — self,
which is *idolatry*. If we ask ourselves the *why* of each
command, we see that they all flow from the first two (no
other gods, no graven image); and they all may be seen to
warn against idolatry. They leave no room for self-will and
self-seeking. Nothing and no one may have the worship,
love, and service that belongs to God alone. Sex can so
easily become an idol. This must be kept in mind as in a
later chapter we approach the seventh commandment ("You
shall not commit adultery") and Christ's interpretation of
it in the New Testament.

In sum, then, the new morality may be seen to possess a basic inherent weakness when one sees that its emphasis on a man-to-man relationship fails to take into account the importance of a man-to-God relationship and responsibility. When its spokesmen argue that we must brush aside the Ten Commandments on the grounds that Jesus said He was giving a *new* commandment ("love one another"), they ignore Christ's own teachings on the commandments. Other New Testament passages that speak of love as the fulfilling of the Law do so in a context that by no means abolishes the specific commands of that Law. (See, for example, Romans 13:8-10; Galatians 5:13-24; James 2:8-12.)

To toss out God's moral law as irrelevant is to throw away the measuring stick that shows how far short of God's standard of righteousness all of us fall. It is by our knowledge of our failure to live up to all that God's laws require that we become aware that we are sinners in need of God's forgiveness through Jesus Christ (Romans 3:19). "Indeed, it is the straight-edge of the Law that shows us how crooked we are" (Romans 3:20, Phillips).

Coming back to the subject of sex behavior, we will see that the Bible does provide clear guidelines and commandments in this important area. But the church has erred greatly throughout history in presenting these guidelines. This is one reason that new morality supporters are wary of any hint of legalism in regard to sex. Our next chapter may help us understand why.

2

The Church and Sex Throughout History

It isn't unusual these days to find statements bitterly denouncing Christianity for its teachings on sex and marriage. Christianity is charged with traditionally setting forth a negative view of the body and looking upon sexual intercourse as something less than spiritual — something carnal and defiling, though unfortunately necessary for the continuance of the human race.

Upon hearing or reading such accusations, many Christians fail to take them seriously or else react defensively and call them the ravings of "ungodly men blinded by sin who are bent on destroying Christianity." There may even be a few Christians who really believe that Christianity teaches that sex is merely a degrading indulgence of the "animal" in man and are glad to see such statements in print! But by and large, too few followers of Christ have given serious thought to an honest examination of these charges, and little effort is made to answer those who have mistaken notions about Christianity's teachings on sex.

There are times when it would be more comfortable to ignore history — to pretend some things never happened. For example, some black teachers recently were criticized for teaching black children the history of their race in America, with special stress on the ugliness of slavery. Criticized for this, one teacher responded by saying that only the truth was being taught and "if white people didn't like it, they should change their history." One might feel like saying the same thing about many aspects of church history — not least of which has been the church's attitude toward sex. But, of course, one cannot "change" history; what has happened has happened. One can, however, *learn* from history. This we must attempt to do if we are to deal responsibly with the matter of sex as seen in Biblical context. Only then can we avoid many of the mistakes made by our forefathers.

Anyone who reads the Old Testament finds it abundantly clear that the Jewish people were not squeamish about the subject of sex. (Modern readers of the *Song of Solomon* who ask, "How did such a 'sexy' poem ever get included in the Bible?" reveal by the very question that they are more informed on church *traditions* than they are on the Scriptures themselves.) Marriage and the family were held in the highest regard by the Jews. As David Mace has written:

> There is a marked contrast between the Hebrew idea that the sexual union of husband and wife was not only blessed of God, but given by Him as a good thing to be enjoyed; and the shadow which, in Christian tradition, has too often been thrown upon the sex life of married people. To cast suspicion upon the wholesomeness of the basic foundation of the married state, and of the normal means of human procreation, would for the Hebrew mind have implied dishonouring the Creator.[1]

Some of the early church fathers did not take their cue from the Old Testament Scriptures. Instead, they were influenced by teachings of Greek philosophy which alleged that matter was evil and that therefore the *body* was evil — a prison in which the soul was kept in bondage until released at death. Thus, the body came to be regarded as an object of contempt. And it shouldn't take much imagination to guess the effect this had on attitudes toward sex!

---

[1]David R. Mace, *Hebrew Marriage* (New York: The Philosophical Library, Inc., 1953), p. 264. Reprinted by permission.

Whereas the Apostle Paul had taught that the Christian's body is the *temple of the Holy Spirit* and should be honored and used to glorify God (I Corinthians 6:19, 20), many early Christians hated their bodies and treated them with disdain. During the fourth century, hundreds of ascetics sought to escape temptation and punish their bodies by living as hermits. The extremes to which they went in their attempts to deny gratification of "physical lusts" seem incredible. St. Ascepsimas wore so many chains that he had to crawl around on hands and knees; Besarion, a monk, would not even give in to his body's desire for restful sleep — for forty years he would not lie down while sleeping; Macarius the Younger sat naked in a swamp for six months until mosquito bites made him look like a victim of leprosy; St. Simeon Stylites spent thirty years atop a sixty-foot pillar; St. Maron spent eleven years in a hollowed-out tree trunk; others lived in caves, dens of beasts, dry wells — even tombs. To suffer the discomfort of filth (most chose not to wash), stench, worms and maggots was considered to be spiritually beneficial and a sign of victory over the body!

For a few of these ascetics, their efforts to eliminate sexual desire seemed to succeed. "Since the time that I became a monk," an old monk told a young man troubled by fantasies of sex, "I have never given myself my fill of bread, nor of water, nor of sleep, and tormenting myself with appetite for these things whereby we are fed, I was not suffered to feel the stings of lust."[2] But others, by denying what God had given and by trying to control sexual desire by self-effort instead of yielding it to God, found themselves more preoccupied with sex than ever before. St. Jerome was greatly puzzled and disturbed by this, as may be seen in this excerpt from a letter he wrote:

> I, who from fear of hell had consigned myself to that prison [a desert wilderness] where I had no other companions but scorpions and wild beasts, fancied myself

---

[2]Quoted in Morton M. Hunt, *The Natural History of Love* (New York: Alfred A. Knopf, Inc., 1959), p. 107. Used by permission.

amongst bevies of dancing maidens. My face was pale and my frame chilled with fasting; yet my mind was burning with the cravings of desire, and the fires of lust flared up from my flesh that was as that of a corpse. So, helpless, I used to lie at the feet of Christ, watering them with my tears, wiping them with my hair, struggling to subdue my rebellious flesh with seven days' fasting.[3]

Many people blame such asceticism on the Apostle Paul's writings. But where this is true, it is because certain of his statements have been taken out of context or used to the exclusion of many other passages. Actually, Paul warned against such asceticism and spoke harshly of those who would forbid marriage and certain foods, all of which were good gifts given by God. (See I Timothy 4:1-5 and Colossians 2:20-23, for example.)

The human body is given great honor in the New Testament — the Incarnation itself being perhaps the most manifest proof of this. The body is "for the Lord" (I Corinthians 6:13-15) and will be raised by Him (I Corinthians 15:35-57). It is to be yielded to Him as a living sacrifice (Romans 12:1, 2), with every member — every single part — of the Christian's body actively surrendered to Jesus Christ to be used by Him and for Him as an instrument of righteousness, not an instrument of sin (Romans 6:11-14). This Biblical attitude is a far cry from that of the ascetics who thought God was pleased if they neglected or punished their bodies. It is the antithesis of misguided notions of men like Origen who felt that self-mutilation (castration) was the surest way to deal with sexual desire.

Whereas Paul spoke of the marvelous way God has designed the human body, with a special purpose for every part (I Corinthians 12:18-24), many early church leaders ridiculed the natural functions of the body. One extreme case was St. John Chrysostom's letter to a young man who planned to marry a beautiful girl. Chrysostom, in an im-

---

[3]Saint Jerome, Epistle xxii (to Eustochium), 7, quoted in Hunt, *op. cit.*, p. 108.

passioned plea that strikes us as absurd today, told the
young man to think what lay behind the lovely face and
figure:

> The groundwork of this corporeal beauty is nothing else
> but phlegm and blood and humor and bile, and the fluid
> of masticated food. . . . If you consider what is stored up
> inside those beautiful eyes, and that straight nose, and
> the mouth and cheeks, you will affirm the well-shaped
> body to be nothing else than a whited sepulchre. . . .
> Moreover, when you see a rag with any of these things on
> it, such as phlegm, or spittle, you cannot bear to touch
> it even with the tips of your fingers, nay you cannot en-
> dure looking at it; are you then in a flutter of excitement
> about the storehouses and repositories of these things?[4]

Believe it or not, that letter persuaded the young man that
a life of celibacy might be best after all!

How different this is from the healthy attitude and joyful
praise of the Psalmist: "Thy hands have made and fash-
ioned me" (Psalm 119:73)! David poured out his heart to
his Lord, saying, "You did form my inward parts, You did
knit me together in my mother's womb. I will confess and
praise You, for You are fearfully wonderful, and for the
awful wonder of my birth! Wonderful are Your works,
and that my inner self knows right well" (Psalm 139:13, 14,
The Amplified Bible).

But such passages were ignored by many early theologians. Augustine thought the processes of conception and
birth were inherently shameful and sordid. His aversion to
the body is shown in a statement in which he speaks with
horror of the intermingling of the sexual and excretory organs.[5] He expressed a wish that God had planned some
other way for human reproduction — something less "embarrassing" than sexual intercourse!

---

[4]Chrysostom, "Letters to Theodore," i, 14, quoted in Hunt, op. cit.,
p. 110.

[5]See Simone de Beauvoir The Second Sex (New York: Alfred A.
Knopf, Inc., 1952, Bantam Book Edition), p. 156.

Overlooking the fact that Genesis clearly states that God created us male and female in His own image and that God looked upon His creation and pronounced it "very good," Christian leaders of the first few centuries after Christ actually taught that the sex organs had been personally designed by the devil and that their "horrible appearance" proved it! Others (St. Jerome, St. John Chrysostom, and St. Gregory of Nyssa among them) taught that God's *original* plan had been for mankind to reproduce in "angelic fashion" (what they meant by this is unclear), but that God had foreseen the Fall and therefore had thoughtfully provided men and women with the reproductive organs "of the animals they would become."[6]

Despite the clear statements of Genesis 1 and 2 that God intended husband and wife to be joined as "one flesh," Augustine tried to imagine some other way that reproduction would have occurred had the human race not fallen into sin — perhaps something like plant pollination. In his *City of God*, Augustine describes in detail what he believes "the act of generation" would have been like in Paradise if Adam and Eve had not disobeyed God.[7]

Closely related to certain church leaders' negative teachings on the body and sex were their low views on *women* and on the institution of *marriage*.

Some historians feel that the anti-feminism of early church leaders might have been a reaction against the growing emancipation of upper-class Roman women. Others feel it was an outgrowth of a harsh strain of misogyny which had found its way into Judaism and was carried over into Christianity. At any rate, women were considered inferior in mind and body; and men who really wanted to please God were instructed to have as little contact with them as pos-

---

[6]Daniel Sullivan, "A History of Catholic Thinking on Contraception," in *What Modern Catholics Think About Birth Control* edited by William Birmingham (New York: Signet Books, 1964), p. 35.

[7]Augustine, *The City of God*, Book XIV, chap. 24 and 26.

sible. That this was directly opposed to the high position
to which Jesus Christ exalted womanhood, and that it con-
tradicted Paul's teaching that in Christ there is neither
male nor female, for all are *one* in Him (Galatians 3:28),
never seemed to occur to many of the church fathers. Instead, woman was called "a scorpion's dart," "a dangerous
species," "an advanced post of hell," who should be ashamed
of her very nature because it was her fault that sin had
entered the world. Tertullian, in his essay, *On the Apparel
of Women*, made one of the severest statements ever addressed to woman:

> You are the devil's gateway: You are the unsealer of
> that forbidden tree: You are the first deserter of the divine
> law: You are she who persuaded him whom the devil was
> not valiant enough to attack. You destroyed so easily
> God's image, man. On account of your desert — that is,
> death — even the Son of God had to die.[8]

Woman was viewed as an evil temptress, carnal and sensu-
ous, who would divert man's attention from God.

In this, as in so many other aspects of the subject of sex
and marriage, the *total* message of the Scriptures was
ignored. That God had made woman for the purpose of
companionship — because "it is not good that the man should
be alone" (Genesis 2:18 ff.) — seemed to be either unknown
or disregarded. To many theologians, woman was made
for one purpose only — maternity. Thus, St. Augustine
wrote:

> If I am asked for what purpose it behooved man to be
> given this help, no other occurs to me as likely than the
> procreation of children. . . . I do not see in what way it

---

[8]Tertullian, *On The Apparel of Women*, Book 1, Chapter 1, in
The Ante-Nicene Fathers, edited by Alexander Roberts and James
Donaldson (Buffalo: the Christian Literature Co., 1886), Vol. IV,
p. 14.

could be said that woman was made for a help for man, if the work of childbearing be excluded.[9]

Other later theologians pointed out that woman's being made as a helpmate to man almost surely *had* to mean for the purpose of reproduction, because, they maintained, in any *other* area a man could be better helped by another man!

If sex was thought to be evil and women were to be despised, it was inevitable that marriage came to be held in low regard. The teachings Paul gave to the early Corinthian Christians to apply to a temporal, local situation (instructing them that they might find singleness more convenient in view of coming persecutions and the soon-expected return of Christ [I Corinthians 7]) were taken to be an eternal and universal law of God. Paul's other teachings on marriage (such as speaking of the husband-wife relationship as an analogy which portrays Christ's loving relationship to His Bride, the Church [Ephesians 5:21-33]) were passed over. Instead, Paul's remark that "it is better to marry than to burn" ("be aflame with passion," RSV) in I Corinthians 7:9 came to be accepted as the apostle's *chief counsel* on the subject of marriage — in spite of the fact that it was written in answer to some specific questions asked by a particular group of Christians living in some of the most immoral surroundings ever known (a thousand prostitute-priestesses "ministered" in the pagan temple at Corinth). These Corinthian Christians were facing unique sexual temptations which were indescribably great and they had written to Paul for advice. Nevertheless, the passage became a favorite with many early Christian leaders who saw marriage as only a remedy — "medicine" for those in poor spiritual health who felt they must give in to physical desire — a condescension to the weakness of the flesh. The Christian

---

[9]From Augustine, *De Genesi ad Litteram*, VII, 3; and IX, 5, as quoted in Sullivan, *op. cit.*, pp. 32, 33.

who was really strong spiritually was expected to choose celibacy.

Virginity was praised with fanatical zeal. The virgin birth of Jesus Christ came to be thought of, not so much as a special sign given by God, but rather as a proof of the "contamination" of normal birth processes. The 144,000 redeemed virgin men "who have not defiled themselves with women" (mentioned in Revelation 14:4) were regarded as positive proof that God delighted in celibacy. It was taught by some leaders that Jesus chose His disciples because they were virgin — a "fact" that seems far-fetched indeed in view of Matthew 8:14 and I Corinthians 9:5. The death of a spouse was looked upon as God's call to sexual abstinence — a "second chance" for a life of celibacy.

In all of this, there was a strange contradiction (seemingly unnoticed) as it applied to women. On the one hand, women were taught that a lifetime of virginity was the pathway most pleasing to God. On the other hand, through an exaggerated emphasis on an obscure and ambiguous verse of Scripture (I Timothy 2:15 — the meaning of which Bible scholars disagree upon even today), women were told that their salvation lay in childbearing!

The Apostle Paul had instructed Christian husbands and wives that sexual intercourse was a normal part of married life and *should not be neglected* except for certain times when *both* husband and wife agreed to abstain for a limited period in order to engage in a special time of prayer (just as food is abstained from in a special period of fasting). Immediately after this, they were to resume sexual relations (I Corinthians 7:3-5). This passage stresses an equality in the relationship and makes it clear that both the husband and the wife have natural desires to express their love through coitus, and neither one should refuse the other but rather look upon his or her body as belonging to the spouse.

A number of church leaders completely overlooked these teachings, it would seem. Jerome would not permit married couples to partake of the Eucharist for several days after performing the "bestial act" of intercourse. "A wise man ought to love his wife with judgment, not with passion," he wrote, adding, "He who too ardently loves his own wife is an adulterer."[10] Ambrose made a similar statement and was quoted with approval by Augustine and much later by John Calvin in his commentary on the seventh commandment.[11]

Jerome told husbands, "If we abstain from coitus we honor our wives; if we do not abstain, well — what is the opposite of 'honor' but 'insult'?"[12] There even emerged gradually among some Christians a strange new form of marriage — "spiritual" or "continent" marriage, in which husbands and wives made solemn pacts of virginity, promising to "keep their bodies for Christ" by not having sexual relations, though continuing to live together, but in some sort of "brother-sister" arrangement!

By the Middle Ages, the Church's teaching on sex had reached ridiculous (and thoroughly unbiblical) extremes. Peter Lombard and Gratien warned Christians that the Holy Spirit left the room when a married couple engaged in sexual intercourse — even if it were for the purpose of conceiving a child![13] Other church leaders insisted that God required sexual abstinence during all holy days and seasons. And in addition, couples were advised not to have sex relations on Thursdays in honor of Christ's arrest, on Fridays in memory of His crucifixion, on Saturdays in honor of the Virgin Mary, on Sundays in remembrance of Christ's resurrection, and on Mondays out of respect for the departed souls (leaving only Tuesday and Wednesday!). The Church sought to regulate every facet of life, leaving no room for the individual's right to determine God's will, nor for the rights of a married couple to decide for themselves

---

[10]Quoted in Hunt, *op. cit.*, p. 115.

[11]John Calvin, *Institutes of the Christian Religion*, Vol. I, Book 2, Chapter VIII.

[12]Quoted in Sullivan, *op. cit.*, p. 35.

[13]Sullivan, *op. cit.*, p. 54.

how the most intimate aspects of married life should be conducted.

Much of this changed with the Reformation. Theologians attempted to search the Scriptures anew to uncover the Biblical teaching on sex and marriage, and a much healthier attitude emerged. While abuses and misuses of God's good gift of sex were warned against, no longer was celibacy exalted and marriage downgraded. And no longer was coitus viewed as a shameful, defiling act. It may be true that, by modern standards, their views leave something to be desired. (For example, the twofold purpose of marriage was considered to be procreation and the remedying of incontinence, with almost nothing said about companionship and affection.) Yet, when one compares the views of the Reformers with many statements of the early church fathers, one must admit that they had come a long way indeed!

And, of course, there were various individual Christians of this period — particularly writers and poets — who did argue for love and companionship in the marriage relationship, and who could view human sexuality as a high and holy gift of God intended for the enjoyment of husband and wife. The sixteenth century poet Edmund Spenser, for example, addressed a series of eighty-nine love sonnets (the *Amoretti*) to his future wife, Elizabeth Boyle. In rich poetic imagery, which could easily remind one of the Song of Solomon, he freely describes his feelings for her and praises her beauty and physical charm while at the same time admiring her soul. His longing for her is never hidden or denied. "Epithalamion," a short nuptial song written before their wedding (published the next year) speaks of the bridegroom's eagerness for the wedding day to end so that he might come unto his love. Then to the "welcome night, thou night so long expected," he says, "Spread thy broad wing over my love and me, that no man may us see." Spenser could with ease blend together his Christian faith with his love for his lady. He saw no reason not to relate divine love and human love. In Sonnet 68 of the *Amoretti*, composed on Easter day, the poet rejoices in Christ's triumph over death and sin and prays that the Risen Lord will grant him and his future wife joy rooted in the redeeming love and resurrection of Jesus Christ. The poem expresses Spenser's desire that he and Elizabeth will be taught new lessons of love by observing *God's* love and that thereby they will learn more of what it means to love their Lord and to love each other.

> Most glorious Lord of Life, that on this day,
>   Didst make thy triumph over death and sin:
>   And having harrowed hell, didst bring away
>   Captivity thence captive us to win:
> This joyous day, dear Lord, with joy begin,
>   And grant that we for whom thou diddest die
> Being with thy dear blood clean washed from sin,
>   May live for ever in felicity.
> And that thy love we weighing worthily,
>   May likewise love thee for the same again:
> And for thy sake that all like dear didst buy,
>   With love may one another entertain.
> So let us love, dear love, like as we ought,
>   Love is the lesson which the Lord us taught.

It is fashionable these days to speak of any inhibitions in the realm of sex as "puritanical." For example, *Time* magazine quoted *Playboy* editor Hugh Hefner's condemnation of puritanism as being as "stultifying" to the intellect as Communism — or any other ideology, for that matter.[14] However, when one actually examines the courtship and marriage patterns of seventeenth-century New Englanders, one finds many contradictions. Thus, we must view the scene from different angles if we want to see anything resembling the total whole.

On the one hand, we see what we have been taught to *expect* to see when looking at Puritans — the harsh, stern, deadly serious, almost ascetic strictness which fulfills the common stereotype. There were restrictions against certain

---

[14]Cover story on Hugh Hefner, *Time*, March 3, 1967, p. 82.

games, Sunday activities, merrymaking, holiday celebrations, and the like — although moderate drinking of beer and wine was permissible. The clothing of women was blamed for contributing to "hainous breaches of the Seventh Commandment," and a 1650 law made it illegal for women to wear dresses with "short sleeves, whereby the nakedness of the arm may be discovered."[15] Church records of one town show that public confession of fornication had to be made by any couple who had a child born less than seven months after marriage. Couples feared the damnation of the infant if they failed to confess. In several cases of premature birth at Plymouth, the wife was placed in stocks to witness the public whipping of her husband. In some areas, adultery was punishable by death, in others by the lifelong wearing of the scarlet letter, "A." Fines and branding with a hot iron were also threats held over those who might transgress sexually.

Some historians feel that the sensational attention paid to sexual errancy only fanned the flame all the more. The detailed public confessions probably brought large crowds who vicariously shared in the offender's sexual escapades. And this unwholesome delight in prying into others' lives, coupled with the morbid, repressive atmosphere, may easily have contributed to an unhealthy preoccupation with sex in many cases.

But that is only one side of the picture. As Robert R. Bell has concluded, "The Puritans were no doubt highly restrictive, but they were certainly not guilty of all the 'puritanism' attributed to them."[16] Morton Hunt has pointed out that the Puritans' emphasis on the sinfulness of sex outside marriage doesn't mean that they were opposed to *sex* as such. In this they differed from the early church fathers who had held such a low view of the body. Puritans had

---

[15]Joseph Gaer and Ben Siegel, *The Puritan Heritage: America's Roots in the Bible* (New York: Mentor Books, 1964), p. 87.

[16]Robert R. Bell, *Premarital Sex in a Changing Society* (Englewood Cliffs, N.J.: Prentice-Hall, Inc., 1966), p. 21. Quoted by permission.

high regard for conjugal relations between husband and wife. In fact, Hunt cites the case of a Boston husband who was brought before his church congregation for discipline because, in efforts "to punish himself for his sins," he had refused for two years to have sexual intercourse with his wife. The congregation looked on this as "unchristian and unnatural" and voted that the man's church membership be taken away![17]

Edmund S. Morgan, after a thorough study of the Boston Public Library's Prince Collection (over two thousand books, letters, diaries, and and other manuscripts on New England history), concludes that Puritan courtship and marriage were definitely not on all counts drab and dull. Real warmth and joy characterized many Puritan families. There were husbands and wives and children who delighted in one another and who delighted *together* in their God. Early love letters make clear that husbands and wives did not fear to express their affection either verbally or physically. For such couples, passion in the sexual expression of their love was not something shameful as some earlier Christians had taught. The only thing the devout Puritan husband and wife guarded against was loving each other so much and prizing one another so highly that they might *forget God* and thus be guilty of *idolatry*. Various letters of engaged and married couples repeatedly speak of how much love is felt toward the loved one, adding, "next Christ Jesus," or "but it must be kept subordinate to God's glory."[18] Morgan writes:

> As a matter of fact the Puritans were a much earthier lot than their modern critics have imagined. . . . The Puritans were not ascetics. They knew how to laugh, and they knew how to love. Yet it is equally clear that they did not spend their .best hours in either love or laughter. They had fixed their eyes upon a heavenly goal,

---

[17]Hunt, *op. cit.*, p. 234.

[18]Edmund S. Morgan, *The Puritan Family* (Boston: Trustees of the Boston Public Library, 1956), p. 16.

and whenever earthly delights dimmed their vision, they knew enough to break off. Few persons today would be willing to learn from the Puritans, for a hedonistic world denies the reality of any but earthly delights. Nevertheless, their books, their letters, and their diaries remain, ready to convince anyone who is interested that a people can live by something more than pleasure and still lead a pleasant life.[19]

The Puritans had strong sanctions against premarital and extramarital sex, but they never pretended that sex didn't exist — which seems to be what *the Victorians* tried to do. Scholars point out that the myth of Victorian purity is just that, a myth. Behind a mask of smug piety, the Victorians practiced a hypocritical morality and seemed obsessed with only one aspect of sexual morals — chastity in women. Pornography, both in books and pictures, was a flourishing trade in nineteenth century England; and one writer asserts that never before or since has there existed such a large number of prostitutes (in proportion to population size) as during the Victorian age.[20] It was lawful to have sexual intercourse with girls over age twelve at that time, a "privilege" taken full advantage of by middle-class factory owners who had scores of working-class girls in their hire. Middle-class women were taught that sexual desire in men was the "beast in human nature," and thus wives pretended to be unaware of their husbands' adultery. Implicit was the notion that prostitution existed for a necessary purpose: it seemed to be a social institution designed to meet man's sexual needs.

In contrast, the woman of this period (both in England and America) was idealized as "the angel in the house," the "guardian of virtue." She was to have absolutely no interest in sex whatsoever, no feeling, no desire. Wives were taught that only prostitutes enjoyed sexual intercourse.

---

[19]*Ibid.*, p. 27. Reprinted by permission of the author.

[20]James Graham-Murray, *A History of Morals* (London: Library 33 Limited, 1966), p. 149.

"Good women" — "respectable" wives — must look on sexual relations as merely a necessary indulgence of their husbands' "animal nature." Coitus was a distasteful act to be endured passively and without interest or pleasure.

Prudery was the order of the day. Books were strictly censored if they were intended for mixed reading; Victorian men did not want their women even to read about sexual topics or have any knowledge about immorality in any form. They must be kept pure and innocent. Even Shakespeare was considered "too coarse" for ladies, except for certain selections. Words such as "womb" or "belly" were, in some cases, expurgated from the Bible and prayerbook. Women were taught that decency means delicacy and were instructed to weep, faint, blush, or shriek in shock or fear if they wished to attract the attentions and protection of the male sex. Euphemisms abounded. The phrase, "in an interesting condition," was substituted for the word, "pregnant." "Leg" was a word not to be used by any decent woman; thus, one had to speak of the "limbs" of the table or piano! The "limbs" of some furniture were covered by skirts because some women wanted to avoid any appearance of nudity! Physicians kept dummies in their offices so that a woman could point to the location of pain without having to show such places on her own body. Some newspapers felt it was too delicate to mention the birth of a child, though marriages and deaths were announced. Pregnant women lived lives of seclusion in their homes, ashamed to be seen publicly in this condition. Once again, sex and the human body had come to be considered objects of shame.

This then is the legacy that history has left us. And it is no credit to the church that artificiality between the sexes, a Mrs. Grundy approach, a hush-hush attitude toward the subject of sex, and embarrassment about the human body have come to be identified with Christianity. An honest quest for the true message of the Scriptures will reveal that such an identification is a serious mistake, because *real* Christianity and the institutional, cultural "Christianity" of history are not necessarily synonymous.

3

Is There a Sex Revolution?

A popular folk song informs us that the times today are "a-changing." Few would dispute this, although exactly how much change is occurring and in what areas raises interesting questions.

There has been, for example, a great deal of discussion in recent years claiming that a revolution in sexual behavior is taking place. Typical was a 1964 *Time* magazine cover story which called what has been happening "the *second* sexual revolution" — a revolution to be compared with the Jazz Age immediately following World War I when the so-called "lost generation" revolted against the Victorianism of their parents.

Other observers of the social scene do not view the sex attitudes and behavior of today's youth as any sort of *revolution* (in the sense of a radical, abrupt change), but they do see a kind of *evolution* (i.e., gradual change in certain aspects of sex behavior and its meaning). Still others point to research that indicates no radical change in rates of premarital intercourse since the 1920's; they feel that if any "revolution" is occurring today it is in the area of *communications*. Sex is written about, surveyed and studied, sung about, and spoken about to such a degree that it seems to pervade all areas of life and simply cannot be escaped. And today's young adults are characterized by openness and a willingness to talk about sex with an honesty

38

that was rare indeed in previous generations. They look at traditional moral standards and ask: Why? What do these standards *mean?* Could they be improved upon — changed in any way? Is there a better way? Modern youth have repudiated the old "hush-hush" attitude toward sex.

What has produced this climate in which young people are endeavoring to hammer out their own code of ethics? There is no one explanation — no easy, simple answer. A variety of characteristics of our age seem to mesh together to form the atmosphere in which today's young adults are laboring to formulate moral standards by which to order their lives. A brief look at some of these may be helpful in better understanding the way in which the younger generation is thinking.

Emphasis on education. In a world where the body of knowledge in virtually every field is expanding at a rate staggering to the imagination, education is of utmost importance. Its value is considered to be incalculable. And one of the most prominent emphases of contemporary education is to train youth to *think* — to reason things out for themselves. Questioning of everything and about everything is encouraged, not stifled. This questioning spirit is carried over by young people into their thoughts on religion and moral standards. To adults who grew up thinking of education as accumulating knowledge passed on by someone else, with emphasis on memorizing facts and assimilating predigested textbook material (and seldom daring to challenge an author's or teacher's viewpoint), it seems disturbing to observe the learn-by-discovery method relished by their youngsters. Many adults wish they could just *tell* youth what to believe and how to behave, and that the younger generation would just *accept* without question. But this cannot be true in today's world. The questions are there, begging for awareness of their presence and for help in finding some answers. Christians must not evade the challenge.

Humanism. Today's generation is sickened by the horror and madness of hatred, bigotry, and war. There is much

concern for human rights — for human dignity. In the ideal-
ism of youth, the cry is for love, for understanding, for
concern for one's fellow-man, for caring about others as
persons, and then formulating one's moral standards on that
basis alone.

Existential questioning. There is great concern with questions of existence today. How are human beings unique?
What is the purpose and meaning of life? Much is being
said and written about the importance of each individual's
acting as a free person — not merely a part of the crowd —
but as a free person making his own decisions, finding his
own meaning, molding his own destiny, choosing what he
himself is to be. Youth is searching in this direction, and
questions about moral standards and meaning in personal
relationships are part of that search.

Equality. Closely related to humanism and existential
questioning is the current emphasis on the rights of every
individual to have a life filled with meaning and to have
opportunities to carve out such a life for himself. Differences in race, religion, and sex are to be overlooked in granting these opportunities; rather, each person is to be accepted
as a person — a fellow human being. Thinking young adults
are applying this not only to such important concerns as
civil rights for blacks, but they are also yearning for
equality between the sexes. Many feel that men and women
have never really learned to know and relate to each other
as persons, because of discriminatory teachings and practices that have set up barriers between the sexes. This, of
course, has implications for sexual standards, and as we
shall see in Chapter 5, it is the main reason for today's
questioning of the old double standard which was covertly
accepted for centuries.

Anti-institutionalism. Young adults are repelled by any
organization that forgets the basic purposes and goals for
which it was formed and instead becomes an end in itself,
cumbered with all the intricacies of gaining and maintaining

power, prestige, and properties. And all too often, the institutional church appears to them to be like that — just one more cold, impersonal organization with contrived schemes and a tightly structured pattern that leaves little room for the free working of the Holy Spirit. They feel it often contradicts its own teachings by all its internal strife and power struggles and by its seeking after goals quite opposite to those of Christ. Many young adults claim that the church is only interested in entangling them in its programs or using them to boost membership statistics, rather than helping them find the answers they're seeking about life. They reject any smug traditionalism that stultifies, that prevents creative thinking, that dampens enthusiasm and vitality, that fears to upset the status quo. Today's youth are deeply interested in religion; they *are* open to discussions on a Christian approach to moral standards. But they want to be treated as persons, not passive pew-fillers — persons desiring guidance in understanding God's will and direction in finding how they themselves, in a mature way and exercising Christian freedom and responsibility as individuals, can work out solutions to their own problems.

Rationalism. Human reason is viewed by many as the highest authority for determining what is best in matters of conduct. Where this is held, the idea of divine revelation is not taken seriously, and Biblical moral standards are not considered indisputable.

Pragmatism. What is the best, most practical, most efficient way of getting things done? This is the credo of numerous young adults in modern, urban, American society. They aren't afraid of change, but welcome it. There is a flexibility, a refusal to be bound by past traditions and ideas if they seem to deter progress, that characterizes youth today. Older adults often feel threatened by any thought of change, because it upsets their feelings of security. Adventurous young people, in contrast, *enjoy* change. They're sold on the idea (sometimes falsely, of course) that the new is always better. This is the "now" generation, stressing up-to-dateness in everything. It isn't suprising then that traditional moral standards are being questioned along with everything else and that some people are wondering if a new morality may be needed for the space age world.

Incidentally, Christians who insist on fondly speaking of the gospel message as "old-fashioned" are cutting themselves off from today's youth and giving a false impression that God, His Word, and His purposes are somehow obsolete. If Jesus Christ is the same yesterday, today, and forever (Hebrews 13:8), it doesn't mean He is "old-fashioned" but rather *forever contemporary*. It is foolish to speak of the "old-fashioned" virtue of chastity, or to tell young people, "I may be *old-fashioned*, but I believe in waiting for marriage." Such terminology can be a hindrance. There's no better way to influence youth to discard Biblical teachings than to label them old-fashioned and give the impression they're outdated!

Honesty. Youth talks much about openness, discarding sham, putting away our masks and being absolutely honest in relationships with others. There is disgust with the hypocrite, the phony, the one who bluffs. And numerous young adults feel that the older generation has not faced sex honestly, nor discussed it truthfully, nor has it practiced what it has preached about it. They are determined not to make the same mistake. They will settle for nothing less than genuineness and realism and have little patience with the moral pretense they detect in the older generation.

Relativism. Today's well-educated young people are aware of the world scene and the varying behavior patterns, standards, and customs of different places and historical periods. Many are asking if there are really divine absolutes to be universally held, or whether moral standards are determined solely by the culture in which one lives. This questioning and idea of relativism is, of course, closely related to the matter of "situation ethics" discussed earlier.

Hedonism. This is the pursuit of pleasure as the chief

end in life. Personal happiness is what matters most. Those who embrace this philosophy of looking for a good time, denying oneself as little as possible, and indulging one's appetites to the full, practice it to varying degrees, of course. But it isn't difficult to see that where hedonistic thinking prevails, sexual standards will likely be affected. Flinging away inhibitions, feeling one has the right to enjoy himself as he pleases, and "living it up" in an eat-drink-be-merry fashion is hardly compatible with restraint in the area of premarital sex.

These then are a few characteristics of modern American society which help make up the climate in which today's young adults are questioning many things that were formerly thought to be beyond questioning. Questions about sex are only one facet of this questioning, but they are a very important part and cannot be ignored. What is often called a "sex revolution" is by no means a nationwide orgy of self-indulgence carried on by a young generation wallowing in the mire of dissipation. Rather, what is happening today (particularly on the college campus) is that young people are taking a new look at sex. They are asking about the meaning of sex and how it relates to love. Young adults talk much about *love* and about having meaningful relationships — not just sex for the sake of sex. They keep searching, wondering how and where they can find the deep rich meaning and loving companionship they desire. Christianity — which is based on love, because *God* is love — should be at the forefront in providing guidance in this quest instead of condemning it.

4

Why Are the Church's Standards Questioned Today?

"I'm going to a doctor to get a prescription for birth control pills," a college student told a friend. "My fiancé and I can't wait any longer. It won't be possible for us to get married until after graduation, and that's a year off. The strain is too great! We've just *got* to be able to express our love sexually."

This girl and her fiancé were both Christians, members of churches which emphasize the Bible as God's Word and stress the necessity of salvation in Jesus Christ. Yet, this couple did not feel that belonging to Christ is incompatible with premarital sex. And their case is not an isolated one.

Many parents and pastors are shocked and disbelieving when such facts are mentioned. But as early as 1949, A. B. Hollingshead's significant sociological study, *Elmtown's Youth*, showed religious leaders to be blissfully unaware of the thinking and behavior of the youth with whom they work — particularly in sex matters. Perceiving this, teens may talk and act one way in the presence of their pastor, Sunday school teacher, or youth fellowship sponsor, but often behave quite differently when with their peers. This isn't to say that evangelical youth are about to organize "sex clubs" or engage in widespread promiscuity. (For that matter, neither is this true of most young people, whether Christians or not.) But it does mean that modern young people are questioning the church's traditional stand on morality, and when Christianity doesn't seem to come up with satisfactory answers, they look elsewhere for guidelines.

One senior at a Western university recently accused religion of using a "scare" approach to morals. He said today's student isn't interested in blindly following someone else's standards — unless he feels there are good *reasons* behind them. After interviewing nearly 2,000 British teenagers, Michael Schofield and his associates reported in *The Sexual Behaviour of Young People* that although many teens gave *moral* reasons for not going further in premarital sex behavior, very few gave specific religious reasons. "Most of the young people we interviewed were not interested in Christianity," said Schofield.[1]

Somehow we have failed to communicate to modern youth the real joy and freedom of living in Christ. All too few young adults understand what Christianity really is! Religious leaders have been content to declare, "Thou shalt not," and let it go at that. But as Pierre Berton points out in *The Comfortable Pew,* this new generation of searching youth will not be satisfied with the church's old answer: "It is wrong." What they want to know is, "*Why* is it wrong?"[2] Psychologist Nevitt Sanford of Stanford University has said that the striking thing about this generation of students is their sincere desire to *search out a moral basis* for their behavior. And they are intensely serious in their attempts to relate their moral ideals to their actions.[3]

Many adults find it disturbing that youth — even Chris-

---

[1]Michael Schofield, *The Sexual Behaviour of Young People* (Boston: Little, Brown and Company, 1965), p. 254. Used by permission of Little, Brown and Company, and Longmans, Green and Co. Limited, London.

[2]Pierre Berton, *The Comfortable Pew* (Philadelphia: J. B. Lippincott Company, 1965), Chapter 5, "Can Christian Morality Be Pre-Packaged?" See especially p. 49.

[3]Nevitt Sanford, "Student Morality: Prospect for a New Ethic," *Old Oregon,* September-October, 1966, p. 16.

tian youth — are asking *why*. They find it easy to conclude from this that modern young people are merely looking for excuses to engage in total sexual freedom. What other possible reasons could lie behind youth's questioning, they wonder. Thus, from pulpit and pen come numerous efforts to set youth straight: "Premarital sex is wrong — *period*. There's no need to ask *why*. It's sin in God's sight, a moral absolute. God says it's wrong, and that's all there is to it."

For some young adults, perhaps this answer suffices. For increasing numbers, it does not. Especially is this true of college students whose educational experience is training them to examine issues critically, to think matters through, to question, to ask *why*.

Religious leaders who *do* make an attempt to answer the why of chastity frequently use arguments that are quickly dismissed by the sophisticated younger generation. Why? Because the emphasis is usually on either shame or fear — and this is why the church's teachings on sex are being questioned and challenged today.

Traditionally, the church has seemed to imply that sex is "dirty," that it's something to be hushed up, something to be ashamed of. Well-educated contemporary youth have little patience with this idea. They point out that they aren't at all embarrassed by their sexuality, and they do not view the human body as an object of shame, but rather of beauty — a view, incidentally, that fits right in with the Word of God. This healthier attitude which regards sex as a natural, normal, and wonderful part of human life is largely the result of better sex education in recent years (whether this occurs through schools, churches, homes, or the increased availability of well-written materials on this subject).

A popular magazine told of one eighth-grader's amazed reaction to a school film showing the uniting of a sperm and egg and the subsequent growth of a baby developing in his mother's uterus. The student said he could hardly believe it — that what he was seeing and hearing didn't seem "dirty" at all.[4] Thus, any approach to morality which hints that sex is basically something vile and degrading cannot hope to catch the ear of the present generation.

However, religious leaders who give the impression that sex *per se* is sinful are becoming a rarity. Instead, attempts are made to warn the unmarried of the dire *consequences* of engaging in sex out of wedlock. This is the appeal to *fear*. Fear of what? Moralists who use this look-what-will-happen approach are most likely to answer along these lines: The girl might become pregnant, venereal disease may be contracted, premarital sex will mean unhappiness in one's future marriage, the couple who engages in sex before marriage will feel guilty, and one's reputation will be irreparably damaged.

The trouble with this approach is that it is apt to boomerang. To young people trained in rational thought, it seems to invite a reply phrased in equally pragmatic terms, namely, that if means were taken to *prevent* pregnancy and venereal disease, and if it could be demonstrated that premarital sex does *not* affect the success of a marriage, and if a couple did *not* feel guilty about having sex together, and if standards changed and our society (like Sweden, for example) came to approve of responsible sex before marriage — therefore keeping one's reputation intact — then, evidently, premarital sex would be all right! This is the danger in this cause and effect approach, even though, in many cases, it is one way to answer the "Why not?" which is so frequently asked today. And of course, there is no denying that there is a great deal of utility in such warnings — any or all of these consequences (pregnancy, venereal disease, etc.) *might* occur for a particular couple engaging in premarital coitus. But the question is, do such warnings really influence the sexual behavior of men and women to the degree that is generally supposed? And if not, what approach should be used in the life of a Christian single young adult?

---

[4]Walter Goodman, "The New Sex Education," *Redbook*, September, 1967, p. 140.

Let's examine the various consequences about which young people are warned and observe some of the strengths and weaknesses in such warnings.

No one can deny the heartache brought about by an unwanted pregnancy in an unmarried young woman — a heartache that not only involves the couple, but their families, their future plans, and, of course, the child to be born. This is not something to be ignored or treated lightly. Obviously, it *does* happen. Statistics of illegitimate births, abortions, and forced marriages among immature couples (who have a high divorce rate), all testify that conception can and often does occur among the unmarried. In some cases, pregnancy occurs among engaged couples who were already planning marriage and who thus may not regard it as the tragedy it would seem to couples who were not contemplating marriage. Facing the fact that premaritally conceived children are an actuality in numerous modern families, the noted pediatrician Dr. Benjamin Spock not long ago wrote an article to help parents answer the questions of their first-born when he becomes aware of "the awkward relationship" between their wedding date and his birthdate.[5]

However, fear of pregnancy seems to be losing the potency it once had as a deterrent to premarital intercourse. (For many young people, of course, chances are still taken and the risks of conception are very real. Nor can it be denied that there *are* those who take very seriously the warnings about premarital pregnancy, and whose awareness of such risks *is* a great factor in discouraging participation in sexual relations before marriage.) But if fear of pregnancy is the *only* support for chastity — the only reason to refrain from sex before marriage, then what is to keep one from engaging in premarital sex *if that fear should be removed?* This is the question being raised among many sophisticated youth today who are aware of the tremendous advances being

---

[5]Benjamin Spock, "Embarrassing Birthdays and Illegitimate Births," *Redbook*, April, 1966, p. 25 ff.

made in birth control. Numerous unmarried girls — particularly of college age and above — regularly take oral contraceptives. In some cases, their mothers are not only aware of this but actually encourage it, feeling a great sense of relief to know their daughters are "on the pill."

One reason for the occurrence of pregnancy among unmarried couples who "knew better" is that they have sometimes been "carried away in the passion of the moment." At such times, the older methods of contraception may have been looked upon as "inconvenient," with the result that no precautions were taken. But newer methods have the potential of changing this. In addition to the pill, current research in birth control holds promise of a "morning-after pill," male oral contraceptives, and anti-fertility vaccines — to mention only a few possibilities. Christians who cite the risk of pregnancy as the chief reason for abstinence before marriage may find their moral standards threatened by such developments.

If fear of pregnancy is not an effective deterrent to premarital intercourse, what about the fear of contracting venereal disease? Modern medical advances have come a long way toward the effective control of vd, and in many respects much of the dread of this terrible disease has been removed — particularly since the penicillin treatment for syphilis was introduced in 1943. However, this is not to minimize the seriousness of the venereal diseases, and information about their symptoms and dangers needs to be disseminated widely. vd is said to be the most serious communicable disease problem in the United States at present.[6] Public health authorities have been particularly concerned about the upward trend in the incidence of vd infection among teenagers — their infectious syphilis rate more than doubled within five years during the early 1960's. Among the total population of adults and teens combined, it is estimated that

---

[6]Lawrence Q. Crawley, James L. Malfetti, Ernest I. Steward, and Nina Vas Dias, *Reproduction, Sex, and Preparation for Marriage* (Englewood Cliffs, N.J.: Prentice-Hall, Inc., 1964), p. 119.

a half million fresh infections of gonorrhea (the most common venereal disease) spring up each year in the United States.[7]

However, despite these facts, fear of contracting venereal disease does not seem to work very effectively as a *deterrent* to premarital intercourse. Just as many people continue to smoke in spite of the established relationship between smoking and lung cancer, many people continue to engage in casual sexual relationships despite warnings about VD. Where reductions in the incidence and seriousness of the venereal diseases have occurred it has been largely because of better knowledge of how VD is transmitted, what precautions can be taken, and what treatment is available — *not* because people have changed their sexual behavior.[8] In the Schofield study of British teenagers mentioned earlier, fear of infection by venereal disease was found to be the *least important reason* (of reasons that could be classified) for teenagers' decisions not to have sexual intercourse. Only one percent of the boys in the sample refrained for this reason, and only two percent of the girls.

There are at least two other reasons for extreme caution in using fear of venereal disease as a prime reason for Christian moral standards in the realm of sex   One is that (as in the case of the premarital pregnancy argument) medical advances could conceivably produce a change in the situation, thereby causing such fear-based morality to fall flat because another crutch has been removed. Breakthroughs in research *could* find solutions to the VD problem — indeed, scientists are at work on this at present. Medical researchers have already made some significant progress toward the development of an effective vaccine to immunize against syphilis. It is not impossible. Thus, Christians must be very careful in making statements to the effect that the spread of venereal disease is "God's way of showing that promiscuity is evil and has terrible consequences." What

[7]Crawley, et al., *op. cit.*, p. 122, and p. 126.
[8]Crawley, et al., *op. cit.*, p. 127.

would happen to that argument if VD could someday be virtually stamped out, much as polio has been?

Another weakness in the venereal disease argument is that it seems irrelevant to those whose conduct is based on a belief in the "permissiveness with affection" standard — i.e., those who believe sexual intercourse is all right between two people who love each other, particularly between those who are engaged to one another. Venereal diseases are transmitted in casual relationships through intercourse with a variety of partners — that is, either the man or the woman must have had sexual intercourse with another person who had the disease and transmitted it to him or her. Prostitutes, pick-ups, and homosexual contacts account for much of the spread of the disease. Promiscuous behavior involving many different sexual partners is the usual way a person is exposed to VD infection. However, awareness of this fact cannot be expected to deter the man and woman who have sexual relationships *only* with that person they plan to marry. Michael Schofield writes: "As the venereal diseases are sexually transmitted, the spread of the infection must involve, not two, but at least three people; one or both of the partners in the sexual act must have had intercourse with someone else. Therefore the venereal diseases must be associated with promiscuity."[9] In itself, the VD-scare approach to the question of chastity has gross inadequacies.

Studies that have endeavored to evaluate the effects of premarital sexual intercourse on one's later marriage have yielded conflicting results. Research evidence has often been contradictory and ambiguous in efforts to find out whether sex before marriage hinders, helps, or makes any difference in overall marital adjustment.[10] So much depends on at-

---

[9]Schofield, *op. cit.*, p. 252. Quoted by permission.

[10]For an interesting discussion on this, see Chapter 9, "Premarital Intercourse and Marital Adjustments" in Lester A. Kirkendall, *Premarital Intercourse and Interpersonal Relationships* (New York: The Julian Press, Inc., Publishers, 1961), especially the summary on pp. 226-7.

titudes, motivation, the type of premarital standards held
(see next chapter), and the kind of relationship between
the sexual partners (for example, a casual relationship for
physical thrills, or a stable love relationship with a future
spouse). And of course, one must ask what is one's personal
definition of a successful marriage. These and many other
factors need to be taken into account. Likewise, some
studies have shown little guilt or regret among many men
and women who have participated in premarital sex. Thus,
religious leaders who base their moral-ethical teachings on
this type of pragmatism (i.e., "premarital sex always results
in unhappy marriages," or "premarital sex always produces
morbid guilt") may find themselves running into some of
the same difficulties as those who emphasize the threats of
pregnancy or VD risks.

The purpose of this chapter has been to help us face up to
some of the complexities inherent in the subject of premarital
sex. Likewise, we have been forced to see some of the
weaknesses in some traditional *reasons* Christians have given
for premarital chastity. However, this doesn't mean that
there are no reasons at all! It only means that many arguments for abstinence collapse (or have the potential of
collapsing) unless we see sex and marriage in *theological
perspective.*

"But can't we leave God out of this?" pleaded a young
man as he tried to persuade his girlfriend to "go all the way"
and was met by her refusal on the grounds of Christian
principles. This is precisely the issue: we *cannot* leave God
out of this. No committed Christian — no person who really
knows, loves, and wants to obey Jesus Christ — can afford
to leave God out of *anything.* The implications of this approach to sexual behavior will be seen in subsequent chapters.

5

Sex Before Marriage

One reason that the church often seems to have difficulty "getting through" to modern youth in providing guidelines for sex behavior is that it so often fails to perceive the way contemporary young adults are approaching the subject.

Traditionally, the church has simply placed all sex before marriage in a single category and labeled it sinful. The issue was settled, and Christians felt certain that nothing more need be said. A man might engage in a brief, depersonalized episode with a prostitute; or he could take advantage of an uninformed girl who "fell for his line" and yielded to his desires without any idea that she was being exploited; or he and his fiancee might find themselves in life's most intimate embrace a few months before their wedding. No matter — as most people understood the church's teachings, all three incidents were *exactly the same*. They were all the sin of fornication, and thus were equally evil because they had occurred before marriage. *Timing* was what made the difference, and little else need be considered.

Then came the rise of humanist thought — the concern for *persons*, the earnest search for *meaning*. Thinking young adults began wondering how the three types of sex relationships mentioned above could possibly be the same. They looked with contempt upon the cheap, body-centered sex represented by the prostitute encounter — just as many de-

plore their elders' leering looks at the go-go dancers at
"topless" nightclubs. And anyone who seriously embraced
humanist values could feel only disdain for the person who
would steal sexual pleasure at the expense of another human
being — a human being whose deepest feelings were tam-
pered with. Today's generation, fervently trying to work
out a value system, scorns sex that is dishonest and sex that
exploits.

"But isn't that *third* category different?" they began to
ask. How can it be said that a couple *in love* are doing
wrong if they mutually desire to express their love in this
way and have no intentions of hurting or exploiting one
another? This is the big question being talked about today
on college campuses and elsewhere — even among young
people from evangelical backgrounds. And they are puzzled
by the church's stumbling efforts to answer, and worse yet,
by the angry censure that so often greets their honest
queries.

The church, without really listening or trying to understand the question, all too often merely repeats its stress on
timing as the only crucial issue; the new morality keeps em-
phasizing *meaning* as that which matters most. Caught in
the crossfire of impassioned charges and countercharges,
Christian young people may find it hard to hear the few
voices that suggest that *both* elements may be involved in
formulating a satisfactory and Biblical sex ethic.

But before such an ethic can be worked out, the sex
situation *as it actually exists* among unmarried men and
women today must be seen clearly in focus. To what extent
is sexual intercourse being engaged in before marriage?
And why? What is its meaning to participants? (In viewing the subject this way, of course, one shouldn't infer that
the "is" determines the "ought to be" of sexual attitudes and
behavior.)

Various studies have been conducted to ascertain the
incidence of premarital coitus, and of these, the Kinsey
studies are the most comprehensive and most widely quoted

to date.[1] The Kinsey studies examined (by interview) the full case histories of over five thousand men and nearly six thousand women. It was discovered that approximately 50 percent of the women entered marriage having had premarital intercourse. Of these, nearly half had had sexual relations only with their future spouse. It was found that the degree of a woman's religious involvement — the intensity of commitment to her faith — had a great deal to do with whether or not she participated in sex before marriage.

Although religiosity was also a restraining factor among men, there was even greater significance in the relationship between *educational level* and incidence of premarital intercourse. In the Kinsey sample, among men whose education had stopped at grade school, 98 percent had participated in sex before marriage. Eighty-four percent of men with a high school education had premarital sex relations. Among men who went to college, the figure dropped to 67 percent.[2] More recent studies have not discredited these findings. Premarital sex is a fact of life that can no longer be swept under a rug of Victorian pretense. Christians must face that fact, try to understand what is happening today and why, and then think through honest (and not overly simplistic) Biblical approaches that will provide guidelines in the area of heterosexual relationships — guidelines that will help youth to incorporate their sexuality with their Christian commitment.

Various efforts have been made to distinguish the different *kinds* of attitudes and behavior characterizing those who participate in sex before marriage. Some authors have made

---

[1]Alfred C. Kinsey, Wardell B. Pomeroy, and Clyde E. Martin, *Sexual Behavior in the Human Male*, (Philadelphia: W. B. Saunders Co., 1948). Alfred C. Kinsey, Wardell B. Pomeroy, Clyde E. Martin, and Paul H. Gebhard, *Sexual Behavior in the Human Female* (Philadelphia: W. B. Saunders Co., 1953).

[2]Kinsey, *et al, Sexual Behavior in the Human Female*, pp. 292-3, 304; *Sexual Behavior in the Human Male*, p. 552.

a distinction between *non*marital sex and *pre*marital sex.[3] *Nonmarital* sexual intercourse would be that which occurs between a man and woman who have no intention of marrying one another; *premarital* sexual intercourse, as used in this precise sense, would refer to those who genuinely anticipate marriage to each other but engage in pre-marriage coitus.

Other behavioral scientists have distinguished between *body*-centered and *person*-centered sex.[4] In his report of two hundred college level males who had participated in sexual relations before marriage, Lester Kirkendall separates types of liaisons into *six* different categories, ranging from intercourse with a prostitute, to sexual relations with a fiancee.[5]

All such efforts point up the contemporary tendency to distinguish between *acts* ("Sex relations took place before marriage!") and *meaning* ("What *kind* of sex relations took place before marriage?"). Christians who cannot face up to this but instead bury their heads in the sand, hoping the sandstorm will just "blow over," are as foolish as those who *are* aware of modern efforts to find new moral standards but who merely dismiss this quest as "immorality and promiscuousness." However, to become panicky and to feel angry and threatened by such attempts to formulate ethical standards is to have a small view of God. Because if one is really confident of God's revelation of Himself through Jesus Christ, if one is really sure of the moral guidance He has given in the Scriptures, if one is really convinced that God *does* have something to say to us in this matter, is there

---

[3]See, for example, Gerald R. Leslie, *The Family in Social Context* (New York: Oxford University Press, 1967), p. 413; and Lawrence Q. Crawley, James L. Malfetti, Ernest I. Stewart, and Nina Vas Dias, *Reproduction, Sex, and Preparation for Marriage* (Englewood Cliffs, N.J.: Prentice-Hall, Inc., 1964), p. 115.

[4]Ira L. Reiss, *Premarital Sexual Standards in America* (New York: The Free Press, 1960), e.g., p. 74.

[5]Lester A. Kirkendall, *Premarital Intercourse and Interpersonal Relationships* (New York: The Julian Press, Inc., Publishers, 1961).

any reason to fear that the entire Christian faith will be toppled because some honest questions are being raised?

Thus, in this book we are trying to approach the subject in the way that modern young adults are viewing it, and we shall endeavor to answer honest questions with the same candor with which they are being asked. Particularly are we concerned with the earnest inquiring of Christian men and women of college age who are seeking *reasons* behind their own moral standards, as well as ways to articulate these reasons to their friends who ask how religious values can make a difference without being "unhealthy" or "repressive."

In *Premarital Sexual Standards in America*, Ira L. Reiss reveals four major standards regulating premarital sexual behavior in our country today: *the double standard* (the belief that sexual intercourse before marriage is permissible for males, but wrong for females), *permissiveness without affection* (premarital sex is all right for both males and females in casual relationships), *permissiveness with affection* (premarital sexual intercourse, under certain conditions, may be right for both men and women if there exists a stable relationship such as engagement or strong bonds of love), and *abstinence* (sexual intercourse before marriage is wrong for both men and women — no matter what the circumstances).[6]

Sex Privileges — for Men Only

The double standard ("boys will be boys") has prevailed throughout history. But with today's emphasis on equality between the sexes, many object to its unfairness. A recent British cartoon summed it up concisely by picturing a girl tearfully telling her boyfriend she was pregnant, only to hear him say that, sure, he knew the baby was his, but he had no intentions of marrying a girl who wasn't a virgin! From this viewpoint, men are evaluated one way and women

---

[6]Reiss, *op. cit.*

another *for the same, identical sexual behavior* — hence, the name, "double standard."

Men who ground their behavior in this standard tend to divide women into two categories: "nice" girls (those who refuse to have sexual relations, regardless of circumstances, until after marriage), and "bad" girls (those who give in, instead of resisting the male's advances). In some cases, double-standard men may even feel that a function of dating is to *test* whether a woman is "good" or "bad." "Will she?" or "Won't she?" (have sexual intercourse) are the questions the double-standard male mentally asks of the women he meets. (Incidentally, male thinking in these terms is widespread enough to have caused concern in recent years when a women's cosmetic product adopted a similar type slogan — though its meaning was, of course, altogether different. According to a television report, several magazines hesitated at first to accept advertisements which featured the slogan, fearing readers would take it as an intentional double entendre.)

The double standard encourages promiscuity and a selfish, body-centered type of sexual pleasure. Some men who hold to it don't want to corrupt "nice" girls — the group from which they hope one day to choose a wife — and so they resort to prostitutes or pick their partners from underprivileged girls of lower-income, lower-status families, who may be persuaded to submit more easily — perhaps by means of gifts, or promises, or a "smooth line."

In some cases, a girl who is shy and not particularly popular (perhaps self-conscious because of a weight problem, or lacking poise because she has never really learned how to make friends and get along with people, for example) is flattered to receive the attentions of a suave campus idol only to find out quite soon that his interest is not in *her* as a person but rather in her body. "Give in and have sex with me, and you'll have lots of fun and dates," he promises her. Such an experience can shock and hurt a girl deeply.

A similar type of cruelty occurs among some double-stan-

dard males who persist in their "testing" even after months
of dating and serious interest in a girl. They insist on their
"right" to prove what type of woman she is. One coed
suffered indescribable heartache when, after months of re-
fusing her fiance's entreaties to have sexual relations because she wanted to save this for marriage, she reluctantly
yielded to his insistence that if she "loved him as much as
he loved her" she would show that love by having intercourse with him. After this sexual experience, he startled her
by announcing that *now* he knew "what kind of woman she
really was" and therefore he was calling off the engagement!
To make matters worse, she later found out that he had
broken off engagements with other girls for the same reason!

The selfish misuse of God's gift of sex, the low view of
women, the deliberate manipulation of fellow human beings
— all these and more are reasons that Christians should have
nothing to do with the double standard. Why should a man
feel that he has a "right" to something that for a woman is
sinful? Why should a girl not have the right to expect
sexual purity in her husband if he expects it of her? Why
should a man feel it is his privilege to try to go as far as
possible with a woman, and it is up to *her* to "guard her
virtue" and police the situation?

Thus, from earliest times, Christians have opposed the
double standard practiced by the societies in which they
have lived. The virginity of *women* before marriage and
their faithfulness after marriage had long been insisted upon
in various societies, but this had been because of a view
that one possessed his wife as property and also a man had
to make sure that no offspring were illegitimate. But for
Christianity to come along and insist on chastity for *men*,
too! It seemed *absurd* and was not always easy for new
converts to accept. However, this was the teaching of the
New Testament and the standard that must be followed.

But it would be unrealistic (and dishonest) not to admit
that the church has nevertheless come to *tolerate* the double
standard over the years; and it is the girl — not the boy —

who suffers the greater condemnation for over-reaching in sexual matters, despite the official position of chastity for both sexes. One need only watch the reaction of Christian people to a premarital pregnancy in their church. All too often, compassion and forgiveness are put out of mind because of fear that this may be mistaken as the condoning of sexual looseness. Since her condition evidences the fact that she had lost her status of virginity, the *girl* — not her sexual partner, even if he belongs to the same congregation — is the one who feels the icy stares and hears the pitiless gossip.

Several years ago, newspaper columnist Abigail Van Buren printed a letter in her "Dear Abby" column which gave a mother's account of how she dealt with a daughter's premarital pregnancy. Her method was to make the girl stay at home and "pay for her sin" by facing the wagging tongues and shame. The mother went on to say that the baby died, but she felt this was "the Lord's way of saying it didn't have a rightful place in the world, anyway." The mother boasted that the experience of facing all the shame and disgrace had taught her daughter a lesson and made sure she "never got in trouble again." The girl never married and is now a middle-aged schoolteacher living far from her hometown. (Miss Van Buren's reply to the letter stated that she felt the mother's "sin" was far greater than the daughter's.)

Sex for Fun

The standard Ira L. Reiss labels "permissiveness without affection" is "body-centered" sex — sex for pleasure and recreation in which neither partner expects anything of the relationship except momentary physical enjoyment. It differs from the double standard in that it permits women as well as men to freely participate in premarital sex with whom and when desired — assuming, of course, that they will show maturity and assume responsibility for their actions, including taking precautions against pregnancy and venereal disease. In many cases, however, such precautionary measures are thrown to the winds as pleasure-seeking teens and adults engage in unbridled promiscuity — such as in the non-virgin clubs or orgiastic sprees that are occasionally featured in sensational news accounts.

A more sophisticated version of the sex-as-part-of-the-fun-of-dating standard is described in various popular books on sex and the single person and of course in the philosophy set forth by *Playboy* magazine. Sex, according to this standard, is merely a natural physical appetite to be indulged and enjoyed — the same argument that the Apostle Paul confronted long ago in Corinth when sex-pleasure seekers defended licentiousness on the grounds that "food was meant for the stomach and the stomach for food" (I Corinthians 6:13). The Bible makes clear the fact that sex is *not* merely a physical appetite in the same sense as hunger or thirst; sex is far more than this — as we shall see in the next several chapters.

Despite numerous articles about a "campus sex revolution," the philosophy of casual, hedonistic sex is really not as widespread as is often supposed. To large numbers of women, the idea of sex is so deeply interwoven with love that they cannot treat it in this "sex-for-fun" manner which detaches sex from a total, meaningful relationship. And many men cannot shake off their double-standard orientation — it bothers them to think of equal sex privileges for girls. Vestiges of the double standard occasionally creep up in the oddest places, such as, for example, in the "hands-off," no-dating-with-customers rules for "bunnies" working in the Playboy Clubs. Asked on a television interview program if this wasn't inconsistent with the "playboy philosophy" of sexual freedom for adults, *Playboy* editor Hugh Hefner replied that such rules were necessary "for the protection of the girls." *Time* magazine reported that *Playboy* even hired private investigators to ask the bunnies for dates, and if the girls accepted they faced the possibility of losing their jobs.[7]

---

[7]*Time*, March 3, 1967, p. 80.

Sex for Love's Sake

The premarital sex standard that Ira Reiss calls "permissiveness *with* affection" is a standard that seems to be growing in popularity — particularly among the college-educated. This is "person-centered" sex, with the emphasis on the necessity of an intimate personal relationship, grounded in love, as the prerequisite for sexual intercourse. More and more young adults, including evangelicals, are asking, "What's wrong with having sexual relations with someone you love? Why can't we 'love' to the fullest extent possible?"

Some adherents of this standard feel that coitus should be permitted only in cases where the man and woman are planning to marry each other. Other adherents define "permissiveness with affection" more broadly and feel sexual relations are justified between any man and woman who have strong affectionate feelings toward one another, even though they have no marriage plans and may, at some later time, "fall in love" with somebody else. In either case, this standard differs from the idea of sex-as-part-of-the-fun-of-dating just discussed in that deep feelings of fondness and a strong relationship must have developed over a period of time before coitus takes place.

Those who advocate this standard resent the assumption that a legal piece of paper or a marriage ceremony has some strange, magical power that suddenly transforms something "nasty" into something "nice." They are repulsed, for example, by the familiar pulpit illustration that compares sex with soil, (i.e., in a garden, the ground is beautiful and purposeful; but in the living room, that same soil becomes just plain *dirt* — because it's out of place). They feel that sex *is* in place when love is being expressed in the intimate communion of a man and woman even if it does take place outside of marriage, and that it is tender and beautiful and not sordid at all. Likewise, they cannot understand why the older generation is so upset with this viewpoint. "After all," reason some young people, "older adults see nothing wrong about making war and killing people! Why should they get so excited because *we* want to make *love?*"

However, many problems and questions cluster about this concept of "sexual permissiveness if affection is present." Can sexual intercourse be placed in the same category of expressing affection as, for example, handholding or a light goodnight kiss? Would such a more casual view destroy something of its uniqueness? Is it a higher view or lower view of coitus that makes it merely another way of saying "I love you" between two people who have a great fondness for each other but have not made the *total commitment that marriage signifies?*

And what is the criterion one uses to determine when he or she is sufficiently "in love" to permit sexual relations? What *is* love anyway? Immaturity (and this isn't merely a matter of age) can cause a man and/or woman to mistake sexual passion for "love" and be swept away in a delirium of ecstasy, only to regret it later when the relationship is found to have little basis other than the physical.

Sometimes a young man professes to love a girl — perhaps even promises to marry her — because he knows she associates sex only with *love*. If he wants sex, he reasons, he'll have to persuade her he loves her and hope she won't detect his insincerity. Often a man will actually hold to the *double*-standard, whereas the woman he is dating holds to a permissiveness-with-affection standard — although perhaps they have never thought of it this way and certainly haven't discussed it together. Then someday after marriage it may be brought up without warning during some heated argument on an entirely different subject. Several women have told of this happening. The husband's long buried resentment of his wife's premarital behavior (whether coitus or perhaps extremely intimate petting which approximated intercourse) suddenly springs to the surface as he shouts, "If you let *me* go that far with you, how do I know how many *other* fellows you were intimate with before we got married?" or "I really lost respect for you when you acted as you did that night when we were dating — you know what night I mean!"

This attitude would not, of course, be present where *both* partners held the permissiveness-when-in-love standard; but few couples would analyze and discuss their views with the openness and objectivity necessary to really know how the other honestly felt. It would be easy to fool even oneself on such an emotionally charged issue. Many couples who sincerely thought they both held the idea that "sex is OK if you love each other," reported disappointment after sex relations took place. Some girls have said they felt "cheap," while their partners have said they "lost respect" for the girl. Obviously such couples were not really committed to the standard they professed to hold.

Kirkendall has shown that *engagement* is sometimes entered and maintained as "a cloak for sexual desires."[8] If a couple theoretically believe in a standard that permits premarital sex *only if engaged*, they might enter into an engagement solely for the purpose of sexual privilege or to satisfy their curiosity about sex without waiting for marriage. Such an engagement (and marriage, if it takes place) is likely to be on shaky grounds. All too often such couples know one another physically without knowing each other mentally and spiritually. Real communication might be nil. A university student wrote to "Dear Abby" to ask if it would be "proper etiquette" to request that her fiance help pay for the birth control pills she was using regularly — a necessity, she pointed out, because they couldn't be married for at least a year. However, said the coed, the problem was that she didn't feel she knew her fiance well enough to feel free to discuss money matters with him!

If one approaches this on humanist grounds alone, there is, of course, another side to this. It would be dishonest to ignore the fact that there are married couples who have no regrets for their premarital experiences, some even argu-

---

[8]Kirkendall, *op. cit.*, p. 163.

ing that premarital intercourse actually strengthened their relationship.[9] However, as was pointed out earlier, the Christian cannot stop with consideration of other persons only; he must take into account his responsibility to and relationship with *God*. And he must look upon the other person similarly. As Helmut Thielicke has pointed out, the other person's value to God compels us to show an attitude of reverence.[10] A Christian may not selfishly fix his thoughts on the importance of the other person to himself alone; rather, he must see that person in his relationship to God.[11] Nor can the *sexual* aspect of life be isolated from consideration of a man or woman as a whole person — a whole person to be viewed in relationship to God and His revealed will. This places the decision to have or not to have premarital sexual relations in an entirely different perspective.

A Christian must especially exercise discernment and caution to avoid being taken in by a certain myth that seems to be growing up around the person-centered standard of "permissiveness with affection." That myth is that such sexual intercourse will not only provide physical pleasure and an ecstatic encounter between two personalities who will discover new truths about each other which could not otherwise be known, but in addition, it will bring about *self-realization* to a degree never before experienced. The person will through sex, it is maintained, explore and discover new dimensions of *himself;* he will be helped to find out "who he is" and what it means to be a human being and to know true fulfillment. Commenting on this idea, Duane Mehl has written:

> Though the sacred writers describe sexual relationship as a kind of "mutual encountering of personalities," they

---

[9]See for example Suzanne Milas, "Why I Believe in Sex before Marriage," *Redbook,* November, 1967, pp. 10-11, and the follow-up letters in the February, 1968 issue.

[10]Helmut Thielicke, *The Ethics of Sex,* trans. by John W. Doberstein (New York: Harper and Row, 1964), p. 97.

[11]*Ibid.,* p. 26 ff.

never speak of anyone discovering "new depths in himself or herself" through sex. In the view of the sacred writers, man does not possess a "depth" except in and through his relationship with God. Or to put it another way: If man tries, without reference to God, to discover depths within himself, he discovers the depths of death. According to the sacred witness, man has rebelled against God and can be reconciled to God only as God forgives him. God, who created man, must re-create or regenerate man before man "finds himself" through sex or through any other form of human activity.[12]

Waiting Until Marriage

Abstinence, according to Reiss, is the fourth premarital sexual standard in America — the one which our nation formally advocates, but which, as various sex studies have shown, is often honored more in word than in conduct. According to this standard, neither men nor women should feel free to have sexual intercourse until after marriage. Some people feel that such a standard is becoming increasingly unrealistic because of the many forces in our sex-saturated society (when even a toothpaste is advertised as giving the user "sex appeal") which seem to conspire together to make chastity difficult if not impossible. Christians are sometimes swept along with this reasoning, forgetting that a crucial part of the Gospel is the availability of Christ's power to enable the believer to resist temptation.

In passing, one other related matter must be mentioned. This is a matter often brought up by those who are questioning the no-sex-before-marriage standard (or at least questioning the hypocrisy of much of it), and has to do with the question: What does "no sex before marriage" mean? Does it mean that one remains "pure" or "chaste" merely by refraining from actual *coitus* — even though extremely intimate forms of petting take place? Harvey Cox

---

[12]Duane Mehl, *Sex and the Silent Revolution* (St. Louis: Lutheran Laymen's League Publication, 1967), p. 12. Reprinted by permission.

wrote of a denominational college graduate who spoke of petting to orgasm every weekend for two years, yet prided herself on her "virginity" because she never indulged in actual intercourse.[13] Robert R. Bell refers to such women as "technical virgins."[14]

In speaking of petting in this sense, one must keep in mind a distinction often made today between such physical demonstrations as handholding and kisses and the very intimate behavior called *petting*. Petting is sometimes contrasted with "necking" because petting is defined as that which takes place "below the neck," including fondling the breasts and genitals. It is the type of heavy sex play that is normally a part of marital intercourse, but it differs in that it stops short of coitus and becomes an end in itself — a *substitute* for intercourse.

It is unfortunate that many Christian young people so misunderstand the teachings of Scripture that they believe they can become "promiscuous petters" with a variety of partners and yet feel they are "preserving their virginity" for marriage. This misunderstanding no doubt results from the church's traditional insistence on chastity, while neglecting to help youth develop a Biblical understanding of *what chastity is*. A standard of continence cannot really make sense until one comes to a realization of the *meaning of sex* as God intended it and to a full understanding of *what marriage is*.

[13]Harvey Cox, *The Secular City* (New York: The Macmillan Co., 1965), p. 210.
[14]Robert R. Bell, *Premarital Sex in a Changing Society* (Englewood Cliffs, N.J.: Prentice-Hall, Inc., 1966), pp. 72-73.

6

Sex and the Bible

The new morality has forced many people to re-examine the subject of sex as treated in the Bible. This examination by persons both in and out of the church has raised some serious questions about Scriptural teachings concerning sex. They are questions that cannot easily be brushed aside — although many Christian leaders are annoyed by them and wish they could do just that. Pat answers, pious clichés, angry retorts, changing the subject, dodging the issues, or pretending not to hear the questions are cowardly ways of handling such queries. Christian integrity demands that we face up to each problem as frankly as possible and with utmost honesty. In this chapter, we'll look together at several of the most frequently cited charges and questions in regard to sex in the Bible.

1. *Doesn't the Bible seem to grant allowance for the double-standard? Doesn't it overlook sexual transgression in men, but condemn it in women?*

This question usually arises because there existed in Old Testament times certain ritualistic tests to determine whether a bride was a virgin, and whether or nor a married woman was guilty of adultery — whereas there were no such tests for males. For example, Deuteronomy 22:13-21 describes a situation in which a bridegroom accuses his bride of not being virginal. He makes a public declaration that he has been cheated, whereupon the woman's parents go to the town elders to offer proof of her virginity. The father insists that his son-in-law has made shameful charges against his daughter, disgracing her. In such a case, the elders require that the accused woman's husband be whipped, fined, and made to keep the woman as his wife, with no divorce privileges *ever*. This is his punishment for having falsely reported that his bride had come to their marriage bed unchaste. However, if the man's complaint was *true*, and his wife's parents were unable to supply "the tokens of virginity," then, under the requirements of the law, the woman was to be stoned to death by the men of the city.

Exactly what these "tokens of virginity" were is not clear. The most common explanation is that they were cloths or a sheet of some sort stained with blood from the breaking of the woman's hymen during the first intercourse. Such tests are still carried out in various areas of the world, particularly in the Middle East. In certain places, the bride's mother rushes to the newlyweds' chamber the morning after the wedding and brings out the blood-stained garment upon which the couple has lain, proudly displaying it to her women friends. In other places, the "tokens of virginity" are publicly shown to wedding guests and to the neighborhood.[1] This is, of course, a highly unreliable test of virginity — the absence of hymenal blood cannot be regarded as positive proof that a woman has had previous sexual relations, and such a test could easily have yielded false results and an unjust punishment.

Another theory is that the "tokens of virginity" may have been special garments worn by all unmarried girls until their wedding day — something like the girdles of chastity or chastity belts worn long ago by certain European women — and that these garments were regularly examined for any signs of disarrangement. Such close supervision by the girl's

---

[1]William N. Stephens, *The Family in Cross-Cultural Perspective* (New York: Holt, Rinehart and Winston, Inc., 1963), p. 225 ff.

parents would make it very difficult for her to engage in premarital sexual relations.[2]

The Bible does not record (to our knowledge) any actual example of a woman's being stoned specifically as a result of the law just described, and it may be that the warning sufficed to discourage unchastity in unmarried women. Also, it's possible that some husbands overlooked the matter or chose not to make a scandalous public issue of the matter, deciding instead to quietly secure a divorce, putting away the woman privately (as Joseph considered doing before God sent the special dream in Matthew 1:18-25).

Numbers 5:11-31 is another passage sometimes cited as an example of the Bible's bias against women in the matter of sexual transgressions. In this passage, the focus is not on premarital virginity, but on a woman's *infidelity* (or alleged infidelity) *after* marriage. According to this law, if a man suspected his wife of adultery and had no witnesses to prove it, he could bring his wife to the priest to undergo a special "experiment" or test which would show whether or not the woman was guilty. In this elaborate ritual, the wife was "set before the Lord" (i.e., in front of the tabernacle, facing the Ark of the Covenant which signified God's presence), with her head uncovered and her hair unloosed. In her hands was placed the special "cereal offering of jealousy, a cereal offering of remembrance, bringing iniquity to remembrance" — the offering that her husband had brought. Then the priest poured holy water into an earthen vessel and stirred into it some dust from the floor of the tabernacle. Curses were written in a book which was then dipped into this "water of bitterness," after which the woman would be required to *drink* the water. First, however, she was required to take the oath which spelled out in detail the two possible effects the drink would have upon her, depending on her guilt or innocence: If she had indeed committed adultery, she would experience terrible pain and bodily

---

[2]David R. Mace, *Hebrew Marriage* (New York: Philosophical Library, 1953), pp. 230-231.

swelling; but if innocent, the water would have no ill effects and she would be free from the curse and able to have children. Bible scholars differ on the meaning of this. Some believe the painful swelling would mean death for a guilty woman; others feel that it had reference to a miscarriage — that a guilty woman would lose the fetus in a spontaneous abortion sometime after drinking the water, whereas an innocent woman would produce a live birth. This latter explanation would, of course, require that the accused woman be pregnant at the time of the ritual (or that she become pregnant shortly thereafter).

What is troubling about this passage is that the ceremony seems unfair to any woman who was falsely accused by a jealous husband who really had no grounds for his distrust. Here there are no punishments spelled out for such a man, as was the case with the bridegroom who falsely accused his bride of unchastity. It would seem that on the slightest whim of a suspicious husband, a wife could be forced to endure a terrifying and shameful ordeal. Indeed, the passage ends:

> This is the law in cases of jealousy, when a wife, though under her husband's authority, goes astray and defiles herself, or when the spirit of jealousy comes upon a man and he is jealous of his wife; then he shall set the woman before the Lord, and the priest shall execute upon her all this law. The man shall be free from iniquity, but the woman shall bear her iniquity (Numbers 5:29-31).

The other question that might come to mind is, what recourse did a woman have if she suspected her *husband* of being unfaithful to *her?*

Both the "tokens of virginity" ritual and the "waters of bitterness" ceremony may seem to pose many difficulties to the modern mind. However, at least three things must be remembered. First, this is part of Israel's ceremonial and civil law, the detailed instructions God gave His people long ago to show that He demanded nothing less than absolute holiness in the life of this nation ruled by Jehovah. These

particular laws, therefore, come under the judicial legisla-
tion intended for a particular time and culture — ancient
Hebrew theocracy. Such regulations pointed out ways the
principles of the Ten Commandments must be applied in
the everyday life of the nation. The specific laws just discussed, for example, impressed the Israelites with the seriousness of God's command, "Thou shalt not commit adultery." It helped them see the importance of the institution
of the family and how crucial it was that marriage not be
corrupted by unfaithfulness. Thus, in addition to checking
lawlessness and preserving order in society, the ancient civil
or social laws served a teaching function.

But as Calvin Knox Cummings has pointed out, "When
Israel as a nation rejected their Messiah and the kingdom of
God was offered to the Gentiles, Israel as a theocratic nation governed by the civil laws of Sinai was no more.
Therefore, these civil laws are no longer binding."[3] And,
of course, on the cross "Christ redeemed us from the curse
of the law, having become a curse for us . . ." (Galatians
3:13). The civil and ceremonial laws of Israel are *not*
requirements for the Christian today. However, the *moral*
law, as summed up in the Ten Commandments, continues
to show man his sinfulness in falling short of God's demands
(Romans 3:19-23) and provides a standard of conduct for
the redeemed child of God who wants to please his Saviour.
The New Testament makes this very clear.

All of this must be kept in mind in evaluating many of
these Old Testament passages. One cannot make authori-
tative statements such as, "the Bible says thus and so about
sex," by pulling out of context certain passages, while neglecting to take into account the times and purposes for
which they were intended and the people to whom these
various laws were addressed.

Second, the entrance of sin into the world spoiled the

---

[3]Calvin Knox Cummings, *The Covenant of Grace* (Philadelphia:
The Committee on Christian Education, The Orthodox Presbyterian
Church, n.d.), p. 18. Quoted by permission.

relationship between the sexes (Genesis 3:16). Rivalry, suspicion, and animosity between men and women, between husband and wife, were some of the most obvious results of the Fall. It is no doubt true that in many cases husbands considered their wives mere property and inferior beings to be ordered about and cast aside at will. Jesus said of the Mosaic divorce laws, "Because of the hardness (stubbornness and perversity) of your hearts Moses permitted you to dismiss and repudiate and divorce your wives; but from the beginning it has not been so [ordained]" (Matthew 19:8, *The Amplified Bible*).

The practice of a *written* bill of divorce (Deuteronomy 24:1-4) is considered by some commentators as being a protection of sorts for women. At least a woman knew what her marital status was if she had such a document; it was better than the uncertainty of an angry word-of-mouth dismissal from the house of a capricious husband who might later change his mind. And the necessity of a written divorce did make divorce somewhat more difficult than it had evidently become in ancient Israel. But we must keep in mind that this was far, far from the ideal of marriage as God had ordained it.

At the time of creation, God brought man and woman together to be one flesh, totally and gloriously united as partners in serving the Lord. That is why Jesus directs our thoughts back to the *beginning* — before man had rebelled against his Maker. Later, we'll examine the implications of this for a Christian philosophy of marriage. Here, however, we want only to note that many of the marriage laws and practices of Old Testament times existed because of "the hardness of men's hearts." ("Because you are so hard to teach," is the way the *Today's English Version* puts it.) They were concessions to the weakness of fallen mankind.

This is no doubt true of the "waters of bitterness" test. It must have been a humiliating experience for the jealous husband who forced his wife through this ritual and then saw no physical symptoms develop to justify his suspicions.

And crude as such a law seems in our modern age, it may have afforded protection for women who otherwise would have been subjected to cruel punishment — even death — if no provision existed to prove their innocence. (In spite of the requirement that witnesses were necessary before punishment could be inflicted, abuses might easily take place in such a sensitive area as suspected adultery.) Of course, for the woman who *was* tempted to commit adultery, this law must have been a powerful deterrent. The very thought of such an ordeal before the priest must have been frightening indeed!

The third thing to keep in mind in reading such passages is that adultery was clearly a sin for *men*, too. Both the adulterer and adulteress were to be put to death (Leviticus 20:10; Deuteronomy 22:22), something that was conveniently overlooked by the Pharisees who brought only the *woman* to Jesus and demanded that she be stoned as the law required since she had been "caught in the very act" — which obviously means that the identity of her partner was known, too (John 8:3-11). The commandment, "You shall not commit adultery," was directed, of course, to men as well as women, allowing no room for a double standard. In fact, part of the tenth commandment is specifically aimed toward *men*: "You shall not covet your neighbor's wife" (Exodus 20:17). Leviticus 18:20 is even more specific: "You shall not lie carnally with your neighbor's wife, and defile yourself with her." In Deuteronomy 22, in addition to some laws already discussed, there are several others designed to "purge evil" from the midst of Israel:

	Crime	*Penalty*
vv. 23, 24	Man has sexual relations with a virgin betrothed to another man. Act takes place in city where woman could call for help, but does not.	Death for both man and woman.

	Crime	Penalty
vv. 25-27	Man has sexual relations with a virgin betrothed to another man. Act takes place in open country, where woman's cries cannot be heard. Considered act of forceful rape.	Death for man only. No punishment for female victim.
vv. 28, 29	Man has sexual relations with a virgin who is not betrothed (cf. Exodus 22: 16, 17).	"Forced" marriage to the girl, payment of the bridal price, and no divorce privileges ever.

Some critics point out that the ancient laws, insofar as the man is concerned, treat adultery only as a violation against another man's property. However, one sees glimpses of a higher view even in earliest times, and certainly later in the Old Testament period as well as in the New Testament. For example, Abraham's deceitfulness which nearly caused an adulterous liaison between his wife and King Abimelech (Genesis 20) was shown to be very wrong for the reason that adultery is a sin *against God* — and this was long before the law was given at Sinai. Chapter 39 of Genesis records the story of Joseph who as a single young man resisted the efforts of Potiphar's wife to seduce him, because he knew that to have sexual intercourse with her would be *sin against God* — not merely "stealing" something that belonged to the woman's husband alone.

In the ancient story of Job, Job says, "I have made a covenant with my eyes; how then could I look upon a virgin? . . . Does not [God] see my ways, and number all my steps?" (Job 31:1, 4), and, "If my heart has been enticed to a woman, and I have lain in wait at my neighbor's door; then let my wife grind for another and let others bow down upon

her, for that would be a heinous crime . . ." (Job 31:9-11).
There are many Biblical passages which warn young men
of the sins of fornication and adultery and are set in contexts that have nothing to do with the property rights of
another man. See, for example, Proverbs 5:15-23 and all of
chapter 7. (Proverbs 6:24-35, however, not only warns of the
spiritual consequences of adultery, but also warns of en-
countering the fury of the adulterous woman's outraged
husband upon discovery of his wife's lover.)

In Hosea 4, God is distressed by the sexual promiscuity
and marital unfaithfulness taking place among His people,
which is symbolic of their *spiritual* adultery in turning from
God to idols. God does not single out women in any "double-standard" fashion, but pronounces judgment on both
sexes: "Your daughters play the harlot, and your brides commit adultery. I will not punish your daughters when they
play the harlot, nor your brides when they commit adultery;
for the men themselves go aside with harlots, and sacrifice
with cult prostitutes, and a people without understanding
shall come to ruin" (Hosea 4:13, 14).

And in the closing book of the Old Testament, God directs
a word specifically to husbands who took lightly the covenant relationship with their wives:

> You cover the altar of the Lord with tears [shed by
> your unoffending wives, divorced by you that you might
> take heathen wives], and with your own weeping and cry-
> ing out because the Lord does not regard your offering
> any more or accept it with favor at your hand. Yet you
> ask, Why does He reject it? Because the Lord was wit-
> ness [to the covenant made at your marriage] be-
> tween you and the wife of your youth, against whom you
> have dealt treacherously and to whom you were faithless.
> Yet she is your companion and the wife of your cove-
> nant [made by your marriage vows]. And did not God
> make [you and your wife] one [flesh]? Did not One
> make you and preserve your spirit alive? And why did
> God make you two one? Because He sought a godly off-
> spring [from your union]. Therefore take heed to your-

selves, and let no one deal treacherously and be faithless to the wife of his youth" (Malachi 2:13-15, *The Amplified Bible*).

When one considers *all* the relevant passages of the Old Testament, there is no basis for unqualified charges that the Bible condones a double standard. And, of course, this becomes even more clear in the New Testament.

2. *How can it be said that the commandment about adultery has anything to do with premarital sex? If only married people can commit adultery, could it be that the Ten Commandments don't clearly forbid sex before marriage?*

First, we must remember that the terms, "adultery" and "fornication" are not always used with precision in the Bible — sometimes they're used interchangably in referring to sexual abuses. For example, in Matthew 5:32 and 19:9, Jesus spoke of a man's divorcing his wife "for the cause of *fornication*" ("on the ground of unchastity," RSV). The Greek word used is *porneia* ("fornication") which usually refers to an unmarried person's participation in sexual intercourse. Yet, here the term seems to apply to unfaithfulness on the part of a *married* person, and divorce was permissible if so serious an offense had been committed. Many new translations substitute words implying *adultery* in this passage. (In fairness, however, it must be said that there are some Bible scholars who interpret Christ's words to mean fornication in its specific sense, i.e., meaning that the wife had entered marriage without the husband's being aware that she had engaged in premarital sexual relations — much as in the Old Testament case discussed earlier where the bride was discovered not to be a virgin. This interpretation of Christ's meaning seems to be a minority view.) I Corinthians 5:1 is another example in which the Greek word for fornication is used in describing a case of adultery.

If the meaning of "fornication" could sometimes be extended to cover any instance of sexual intercourse between two people *who were not married to each other*, regardless of their individual marital status (an admissible meaning which is still mentioned in modern English dictionaries in regard to present-day usage of the word, "fornication"), then it might likewise be held that the word "adultery" could be used in a similar fashion. The strong possibility that this is so in regard to the seventh commandment may be inferred from Jesus' comments on this commandment in Matthew 5:27-30.

Here Jesus does not appear to be addressing married persons alone. He says, "Every one who looks at a woman lustfully has already committed adultery with her in his heart." The words are "every one" — not "every married person." He says, "looks at a woman" — not "looks at a *married* woman." In this passage, there is no thought that a man's offense would be against another man's "property rights" to the exclusive possession of his wife's sexuality. Rather the implication is clear throughout this section of Scripture that disobeying God's commands in regard to sex must be considered *sin*, an offense against a Holy God. "Adultery," as used here, then, would seem to have the same meaning as the sense in which "fornication" was used above, i.e., sexual relations between any man and woman who are not married to each other. If Jesus Christ extended the meaning of the seventh commandment thus to cover all instances of unchastity (in thought as well as in act), can we do less?

Incidentally, this teaching was not intended for men only; the words of Jesus apply to women as well. The Bible never ignores the fact that women have sexual desires, too, and that women may sometimes be the ones to initiate sexual relations that are contrary to God's plans. Examples of this are Lot's daughters (Genesis 19:30-38), Potiphar's wife (Genesis 39:7 ff.), and the woman whose husband was away on a journey (Proverbs 7:10-27).

One further word is in order as regards the commandment, "You shall not commit adultery," as originally given in Exo-

dus 20:14 (and setting aside for a moment Christ's exposi-
tion as discussed above). A high proportion of the sexual
offenses of the Old Testament period no doubt fell precisely
into the category of *adultery* — in the usual, specific, more
limited sense of that word. This was because marriage
generally occurred for both boys and girls shortly after they
reached the age of puberty.[4] There was little time or feeling
of "need" for sexual relations before marriage in the early
Hebrew culture. Opportunity for sexual expression in marriage usually concurred with the awakening of the sexual
powers during adolescence. Thus, one finds in the Bible
frequent expressions such as "the wife of your youth" (Proverbs 5:18; Isaiah 54:6; Malachi 2:14-16)), "companion of her
youth" (Proverbs 2:17), "bridegroom of youth" (Joel 1:8),
and "children of youth" (Psalm 127:4) — all implying that
marriage took place at an early age.

Young people who weren't married were usually at least
betrothed. Parental arrangements were the normal custom;
and in the betrothal ceremony, a couple entered into a
binding covenant whereafter they belonged to one another
only. Betrothal and marriage were virtually synonymous.
As we saw in Deuteronomy 22:23 ff., no distinction was made
between a wife and a betrothed maiden — for a man to have
sexual relations with a young woman who was betrothed
was in the eyes of the law exactly the same as sexual relations with another man's wife. Hence, opportunities to commit the sin of adultery were far more prevalent than opportunities to commit the sin of fornication (in the cus-
tomary, specific sense of each word), since through marriage
— or at least betrothal — men and women were considered
to be in the state of wedlock from an early age. As we saw
earlier, sexual relations between two persons who were *unmarried* (and unbetrothed) required that they must marry
one another (Deuteronomy 22:28; Exodus 22:16, 17).

In sum, then, we may say that, according to the teaching
of Christ, the seventh commandment does have implications

---

[4]Mace, *op. cit.*, pp. 143-4.

for premarital as well as extramarital sexual relations. Also,
it is worthy of note that in the Jewish rabbinical writings,
sex before marriage was condemned as immorality in teachings which explained and commented on God's moral law
as revealed in Scripture;[5] and this has likewise been the
traditional interpretation of the seventh commandment
throughout the history of the Christian church. The *intent*
of the command would seem to cover the misuse of sex in
any form.

3. *Does the Bible make any distinction between premarital sex of a casual sort, with no strong emotional at-
tachment, and premarital sex between a man and woman
who love each other?*

The Scriptures are very clear in condemning casual, body-
centered sex — sex with just anyone purely for the sake of
pleasure and thrills. This doesn't meant that there is a denial
that sex is pleasurable, nor does it mean that the *enjoyment*
aspect of sex is somehow wrong or evil. Sex is one of God's
good gifts; but like any other of His gifts, its use must take
into account one's responsibility to God and to others. Sex
must not be considered as merely a plaything for selfish
indulgence. Thus, promiscuity is shown throughout the
Bible to be incompatible with personal holiness and contrary to the will of God.

> This is the will of God, that you should be holy; you
> must abstain from fornication; each one of you must learn
> to gain mastery over his body, to hallow and honour it,
> not giving way to lust like the pagans who are ignorant of
> God; and no man must do his brother wrong in this mat-
> ter, or invade his rights, because, as we told you before
> with all emphasis, the Lord punishes all such offences.
> For God called us to holiness, not to impurity. Anyone

---

[5]Max L. Margolis, "Adultery," *The International Standard Bible
Encyclopedia*, ed. by James Orr (Grand Rapids: Wm. B. Eerdmans
Publishing Co., 1939), Vol. I, p. 63.

therefore who flouts these rules is flouting, not man, but God who bestows upon you his Holy Spirit.

I Thessalonians 4:3-8, NEB

Jesus warned against both fornication and adultery (indicating that He was very explicit in addressing both single and married persons in regard to sexual transgressions), and included both fornication and adultery in His list of evil things which come out of the heart and defile a person (Mark 7:21; Matthew 15:19). Other New Testament passages likewise point out that a hedonistic philosophy of premarital sex is out of bounds for anyone who really wants to please God.

Fornication and indecency of any kind, or ruthless greed, must not be so much as mentioned among you, as befits the people of God. No coarse, stupid, or flippant talk; these things are out of place; you should rather be thanking God. For be sure of this: no one given to fornication or indecency or the greed which makes an idol of gain, has any share in the kingdom of Christ and of God.

— Ephesians 5:3-5, NEB

Were you not raised to life with Christ? Then aspire to the realm above, where Christ is, seated at the right hand of God, and let your thoughts dwell on that higher realm, not on this earthly life. I repeat, you died; and now your life lies hidden with Christ in God. When Christ, who is our life, is manifested, then you too will be manifested with him in glory. Then put to death those parts of you which belong to the earth — fornication, indecency, lust, foul cravings, and the ruthless greed which is nothing less than idolatry. Because of these, God's dreadful judgment is impending.

— Colossians 3:1-6, NEB

Those who belong to Christ Jesus have crucified their old nature with all that it loved and lusted for. If our lives are centered in the Spirit, let us be guided by the Spirit.

— Galatians 5:24, 25, Phillips

> If you are guided by the Spirit you will not fulfill the
> desires of your lower nature. . . . Anyone can see the kind
> of behaviour that belongs to the lower nature: fornica-
> tion, impurity, and indecency; idolatry and sorcery; quar-
> rels, a contentious temper, envy, fits of rage, selfish ambi-
> tions, dissensions, party intrigues, and jealousies; drinking
> bouts, orgies, and the like. I warn you, as I warned you
> before, that those who behave in such ways will never
> inherit the kingdom of God.
>
> — Galatians 5:16, 19-21, NEB

Perhaps the most explicit warning against sexual promiscuity is found in I Corinthians 6:12-20. There the Christian
is told that his body is for the Lord — to be used by Christ
and controlled by Christ. When the Corinthians pointed
out that their stomachs were made for food and implied that
the existence of an appetite proved the lawfulness of its
gratification, the Apostle Paul made it clear that sex is not
merely a physical appetite. Sexual intercourse involves the
totality of a person's being. As Harvey Cox has pointed out,
"Saint Paul saw the striking fact that as human beings we
both *have* and *are* bodies. . . . Paul saw that sex — unlike
excretion, for example — is not simply a physiological but
also a 'bodily' (somatic) activity. It involves us at the deepest levels of our personal identity."[6]

The Corinthians' argument that "food is meant for the
stomach and the stomach for food" will not stand when
one sees the distinction between the organs of nutrition and
that body which is part of our permanent individuality.
The digestive organs will perish — for the time will come
when the Christian no longer needs food for sustenance.
But whereas the stomach is transitory, the body is eternal
and sacred. This differentiation between the "soma" (the
body as a sound whole) and the stomach (representing
earthly, temporal biological craving) must be kept in mind.

---

[6]Harvey Cox, *The Secular City* (New York: The Macmillan
Co., 1965), p. 211.

The purpose of the body (for the Lord), its destiny (resurrection), its function (the temple of the Holy Spirit), its proprietorship (owned by God), and its aim (to glorify God) are not matters that any Christian can dismiss lightly.

Sexual intercourse *does* involve one's "body as a sound whole." It *does* involve the very core of one's being. Something happens between two persons on more than a physical level in this most intimate of acts; in some mysterious sense, "the two become one flesh," to use the Biblical expression. The relationship somehow reaches deeper than might be expected. It isn't something that can be toyed with. Thus, the Scripture says to "flee fornication" — *shun* immorality, stay away from promiscuity. We'll look into further reasons for this in the following chapters.

But this still leaves a big question unanswered. What about the standard that says "sex is OK when you're in love"? Does the Bible call this fornication, too? The new morality has raised this question in the minds of many thoughtful young adults. Some Christian students who have studied the derivation of the word translated *fornication* in the New Testament point out that it is the Greek "porneia," which refers, they feel, only to *harlotry* or prostitution. (Our English word, "pornography," from the same root, literally means "writing about harlots.") The word "fornication" itself springs from a Latin root meaning "arch, basement, brothel" — that is, the place where illicit sex acts took place.

The meaning of both the Greek "porneia" and the English "fornication" were, however, extended to cover *all instances of sex before marriage* and referred especially to promiscuity. As we saw above, promiscuity is clearly forbidden in the Scriptures. This raises the question: just what *is* promiscuity? Dictionaries define it as indiscriminate sexual relations with a variety of partners on a casual basis. The Biblical ideal (reasoning from the "one flesh" idea) is that sexual relations should take place only with one's life partner. The sex relationship is a unique fusion too special and too meaningful to be experienced with someone to whom one is not totally committed to share one's entire life with. Thus, sexual intercourse may not be viewed (insofar as the Bible is concerned) as merely a mutually pleasant way to express affection toward someone for whom one has "feelings of love" or fondness. Adherents of the premarital-sex-is-all-right-when-in-love standard may not always be able to define "love" except in a hazy, romantic sense, based on *feelings* which may (and often do) change. Thus, although they may not agree with the sex-with-just-anyone-for-a-good-time standard, they may nonetheless "fall in love" with many *different* individuals at *different* times and justify intercourse on the basis of that "love" — thereby, in essence, placing themselves in the category of "promiscuity" (Biblically speaking).

But what about an engaged couple? Here is a Christian couple who have no intention of breaking their engagement, who are thoroughly committed to one another, who definitely plan to marry. Would they, they wonder, be doing wrong to express their love through sexual relations in advance of the wedding? Wouldn't they be avoiding the *promiscuity* the Bible warns about and instead be fulfilling the "two becoming one flesh" ideal, sharing their bodies *only* with the partner with whom there will be a lifelong sharing? Is the event of the marriage ceremony the all-deciding factor that determines *when* sex relations may take place? Some such couples are asking: "Why can't we consider ourselves married even if no one else does? After all, we *feel* married." (These questions *are* being voiced among evangelical young people, and the issue is not helped by evading it — despite the fact that many Christians are shocked that such matters even come up.)

This question will be explored at length in the next chapter as we discuss what *marriage* is. However, at this point, perhaps a word is in order to challenge a statement frequently made these days to the effect that the Bible is totally silent about the matter of sex relations between those who plan to marry anyway but find it difficult to wait.

It is entirely possible that St. Paul's oft-quoted (and oft-

criticized) statement in I Corinthians 7:9 that it is "better
to marry than to burn" (or "be aflame with passion," RSV)
may be particularly applicable to the engaged couple who
find their desire for one another difficult to control. "If any
one thinks that he is not behaving properly toward his
betrothed, if his passions are strong, and it has to be, let him
do as he wishes; let them marry — it is no sin" (I Corinthians
7:36). For a complete understanding of this passage, one
must take into account customs of the time and place to
which the apostle addressed himself. But here we want only
to note that regardless of the betrothal practices of the
times, *implicit is the standard that the full sexual expression
of love is to be reserved for marriage.* There is no hint that
if passions are strong, if sexual desire is great, then one
should "give in" to that urge and find relief from sexual
tensions. Rather, "let them marry" is Paul's counsel to the
betrothed man and woman in such a situation. "If you cannot restrain your desires, go on and marry — it is better to
marry than to burn with passion" (I Corinthians 7:9, TEV).
Those who reply, "But we're not ready for marriage yet,
even though we're ready for sex," should do some serious
thinking on both the meaning of sex and the meaning of
marriage.

7

What Is Marriage?

To many people, the title of this chapter may seem foolish. Doesn't *everybody* know what marriage is, when and how it occurs, what it consists of, what it means? However, when one begins seriously to think through these questions, the answers may not be so simple as originally supposed.

An understanding of the nature of marriage is crucial in clarifying moral standards and finding a rationale for Christian sexual ethics. This is true for at least two reasons: (1) Marriage is a *social* matter. It is an arrangement that not only includes an individual man and woman, but also other people — the "larger society" in which the couple live. And (2) marriage as God intended it has theological significance — it involves the couple and God.

Let's look at these two ideas concerning marriage and see how they may provide some insight into the matter of sex morals.

Marriage in Social Perspective

If American society is characterized by anything, it is our strong stress on *individualism*. We believe that the individual should have maximum freedom to make his own decisions. Unfortunately, this strong ideology often blinds Americans to the fact of the *indivisibility* of human beings from one another. John Donne's oft-quoted words, "No man is an island, entire of itself," are just as true now as

86

they were in the seventeenth century. The great humanitarian and social concerns of our day are evidence of our increasing awareness of the interdependence and indivisibility we share with others, and a repudiation of naive individualism.

Marriage is often thought of in an extremely individualistic fashion. Two people love each other, so they marry — it's as simple as that. But is it? Even "B" movies and television series show an awareness of at least two social linkages that impinge on marriage — parents and friends. For in spite of the desire to be free and make one's own choices, most young people, by the time they're ready to marry, have gotten their parents' approval to do so. Not that they couldn't legally marry without such consent (if they meet the age requirements of their state), but there are strong social pressures to have the parents "in" on the wedding — to have their blessing and general good will. Furthermore, in some cases, parents give substantial financial aid to young couples just getting started, and this cannot be ignored.

And what of friends? Young men and women are keenly aware of the reaction of friends when they mention the name of some prospective date, and these kinds of subtle but powerful sanctions have much to do with shaping the course of a courtship and the ultimate choice to marry or not to marry a particular person. The process of consulting peers on the "worth" of various members of the opposite sex is a continuous one. Almost everyone who marries seeks the counsel of his friends in subtle (and sometimes open) ways. Men and women want to sense the opinions of their friends in this crucial decision. And the fact is that most studies of divorce show that people who eventually dissolve their marriages are, among other things, likely to be those who rejected the advice of parents and/or friends *not* to marry a certain person.

Marriage then is a social relationship as well as an individual relationship. It is the concern of *others* besides the male and female involved. In fact, no one is really married *unless at least one other person knows about it.*

Marriage is the *socially permitted* cohabitation of male and female. As Pieter de Jong puts it:

> Sex in the human is never a merely physical concern. Nor is it a purely private matter; for sex on the level of man inevitably has social implications. What goes on between the partners is a concern of society as a whole. Humanization demands that the total union of two persons be made public and protected by marriage as an institution.[1]

To be valid from the social point of view, marriage must be a public — not a private — affair. Those who have sexual intercourse before conforming to whatever public disclosure their societies require cannot reason that they are now married.

The form of this public disclosure may vary from culture to culture. In early Old Testament times, it involved an agreement between the parents of the bride and the parents of the groom and included the custom of exchanging gifts. Thus, for example, when Isaac and Rebekah entered their tent together after these customs had been fulfilled (Genesis 24), they were recognized to be husband and wife by the society in which they lived, even though no mention is made of spoken nuptial vows or wedding ceremonies as we know them today.

Later in Hebrew culture, more elaborate ceremonies surrounded marriage, including the wearing of special attire and a public procession in which the bridegroom brought the bride to his home for several days of festivities. The legal marriage contract had actually been entered at the time of the *betrothal* many months before the wedding and was looked upon as a binding covenant between the man and woman and both families. However, the marriage was

---

[1]Pieter de Jong, "Christian Anthropology: A Biblical View of Man," in John Charles Wynn, Ed., *Sex, Family, and Society in Theological Focus* (New York: Association Press, 1966), pp. 84-85. Reprinted by permission.

not considered *consummated* until the couple began to reside together and had their first sexual union. (Thus, the distinction between *betrothing* a wife and *taking* a wife in Deuteronomy 20:7.) Usually, this consummation took place the first night of the wedding festivities in a special tent or room called the bridechamber. The rituals surrounding proof of virginity occurred at this time.

The ancient Romans had various types of wedding ceremonies, but the most important part of all of them seems to have been the joining of hands by the couple in the presence of witnesses, thereby declaring publicly their desire to join their lives together. At this time, there were sometimes brief words of consent spoken, prayers and sacrifices offered to the gods, a sharing by the bride and groom of a cake that had first been dedicated to Jupiter or some of the other gods, then congratulations by the witnesses of the wedding. If the ceremonies occurred at the bride's home, the groom took his bride away to his home immediately afterwards. There was much gaiety, singing, and a spirit of festivity as the wedding procession passed through the crowded streets.[2]

The Greeks, too, celebrated marriage ceremonies with feasting. Their wedding feasts began with a "handle kiss" by the bride and groom; each held the other's ears while their lips touched. Since the Greeks considered the onion to have the qualities of a love potion, it was not uncommon for onions to be eaten before the wedding kiss took place![3]

The method by which a man and woman enter the wedded state still varies from culture to culture today. But what they all have in common is some sort of public disclosure that a new husband-wife unit has been formed — that the status of wedlock has been entered by a particular

---

[2]Stuart A. Queen, Robert W. Habenstein, and John B. Adams, *The Family in Various Cultures* (Philadelphia: J. B. Lippincott Co., 1961), pp. 164-166.

[3]Ira L. Reiss, *Premarital Sexual Standards in America* (New York: The Free Press of Glencoe, 1960), pp. 46-47.

couple. Some of the ways this public announcement is made may seem strange to Americans. For example, anthropologists tell us of an unusual marriage ritual among the Kwoma of New Guinea. When a boy and girl are interested in marriage, the girl moves in with the boy's family for a time of becoming better acquainted. During this period, the girl cooks her own food, while the boy's mother and sisters prepare the food for the others of the household. However, when the mother feels the time has come for the marriage to take place (and this she alone decides on the basis of how pleased she is with the girl and if she perceives that her son is satisfied also), she tells the betrothed to prepare the young man's supper some time while he is away from the house. When he returns and unsuspectingly begins eating his food, his mother announces that *now he is married* — because he is eating food his betrothed has prepared. Upon hearing this, the young man is supposed to rush outside shouting how terrible the food tastes. And this is the public declaration that he is now a married man! The couple begin living together as husband and wife immediately after this.[4]

Why is a public declaration inherent in the very idea of marriage? The answer is simple — protection. Protection (1) for the partners involved, (2) for any future children, (3) for peers, and (4) for society as a whole.

As far as the partners are concerned, there are psychological, spiritual, and economic investments involved in living together and having sexual access. Public affirmation of mutual commitment is more apt to protect these investments, to increase the probability of long-range growth, and to reduce the probability of exploitation of one by the other. For example, the economic aspects of marriage are often overlooked by young people, but there are reams of laws governing property and inheritance which many people

---

[4]William N. Stephens, *The Family in Cross-Cultural Perspective* (New York: Holt, Rinehart, and Winston, Inc., 1963), pp. 221-222.

don't even know exist until death or divorce thrust them into view.

Second, unborn children have the right to be guaranteed a legitimate status, as well as a reasonable probability of emotional and economic stability.

Third, other people have the right to know that a man and woman are pledged to one another. And, therefore, no one else has any right to sexual relations with either one of them. (See Genesis 12:10-20; 20:1-18; and 26:6-11 in this regard.)

Suppose, however, a man and woman let it be known to their friends that they are living together but have not conformed to the demands of their society in regard to *legitimate* public declaration (whether that involves licenses, marriage contracts, particular types of ceremonies performed by designated authorities, or whatever). This takes care of Item 3 above, but still leaves Items 1, 2, and 4.

No society can or does permit sexual behavior to go uncontrolled. If sex and reproduction are random, promiscuous, and fluid in their structure, the basic social order of that society — whether primitive or mass society — is threatened. Even those who argue for "trial marriages" recognize this requisite of making these public. While all societies tolerate some deviation from sexual control, there are limits beyond which no society can go and still maintain its stability or order.

Therefore, while marriage, of course, involves sexual intercourse, sexual access in itself does not mean marriage. The elements of sexual access *and* economic sharing (or bed and board) *and* societal recognition are inextricably intertwined in defining marriage. If a man and woman go to bed together without telling their society they are doing so, they may consider themselves many things, but they cannot consider themselves *married*.

In passing, mention might be made of a case that may at first appear to be an exception to this. Among the Wapisiana of British Guiana in South America, cohabitation is defined as marriage, thus eliminating the possibility of coitus be-

tween two unmarried people (because the very act of intercourse makes the couple husband and wife). However, this
is not a promiscuous society by any means. Marriage is
monogamous, and up until the time of marriage, there is
maintained strict segregation of the sexes except in the
presence of chaperones. When a man and woman decide to
begin living together, it is publicly acknowledged. Cohabitation in this society means taking on all the obligations
and responsibilities of marriage, not merely obtaining the
privilege of sex relations.[5] Thus, even this form of marriage
is not an individual, private matter; rather, society's requirements are met, and social order is maintained.

Marriage in Theological Perspective

Whenever Jesus was asked about marriage, He directed
His listeners back to the beginning — back to the time when
the first man and woman were bound together in that unique
relationship which marked the establishment of the institution of marriage according to God's plan. In Matthew 19:
1-12 (together with Genesis 2:18-25), we see the ideal that
Jesus Christ set forth for those who are called by His name.

It might be well to start out with Matthew 19:11 ("Not
all men can receive this precept, but only those to whom it
is given") — a verse usually thought to have special reference to the verse that follows it. But it is just as possible
that Christ was relating it to His preceding statements —
teachings which, to the disciples, seemed to set forth an
ideal of marriage virtually impossible to attain. In explaining
this verse, William Barclay writes:

> What Jesus is really saying is this — *Only the Christian
> can accept the Christian ethic.* Only the man who has
> the continual help of Jesus Christ and the continual
> guidance of the Holy Spirit can build up the personal
> relationship which the ideal of marriage demands. Only

---

[5]Clellan S. Ford and Frank A. Beach, *Patterns of Sexual Behavior*
(New York: Harper and Row, 1951), p. 183.

by the help of Jesus Christ can a man develop the sympathy, the understanding, the forgiving spirit, the considerate love, which true marriage requires. Without the help of Jesus Christ these things are plainly impossible. The Christian ideal of marriage involves the prerequisite that the partners to marriage are Christian. . . . [Christ's] teaching only becomes possible in the conviction that He is not dead, but that He is present here to help us carry it out. The teaching of Christ demands the presence of Christ: otherwise it is only an impossible — and a torturing — ideal.[6]

With this in mind, let's look at the ideal to which Christ directs us.

Jesus stressed that God created mankind in two sexes. "Have you not read that he who made them from the beginning made them male and female" (Matthew 19:4). Christ made it clear that human sexuality was designed by God — a wondrous part of the Creator's handiwork which He pronounced *very good.* Sex is therefore not to be despised, nor disregarded, nor defiled, nor deified, but is to be reverently accepted as a gift of God to be received with thanksgiving, and enjoyed, and used for His glory. The "maleness" of man and the "femaleness" of woman originated in the mind of God; therefore, both sexes need to seek out His plan as to how they should relate to one another, not as mere bodies, but as whole persons — human beings who are alike, yet different, with neither sex being inferior nor superior, but equal in the sight of God.

God created mankind — both male and female — in His image. "When God created man, he made him in the likeness of God. Male and female he created them, and he blessed them and named them Man when they were created" (Gene-

---

[6]From *The Gospel of Matthew, Vol. 2,* translated and interpreted by William Barclay. (Published in the U.S.A. by the Westminster Press, 1959, and in Edinburgh, Scotland by the St. Andrew Press, 1957), pp. 227-228. Used by permission of both publishers.

sis 5:1, 2). This bearing of the image of God distinguishes
human life from all other forms of life. A serious contem-
plation of all that this means cannot help but have an effect
on sexual attitudes and conduct both before and after marriage, as well as on all other aspects of man-woman relationships. When one is conscious that the partner is made in
the image of God, and that one must consider that person
in relation to God, self-centered exploitation, manipulation,
or domination of a woman or man becomes mockery against
God.

*God instituted marriage as a unique means of companion-
ship.* "The Lord God said, 'It is not good that the man
should be alone; I will make him a helper fit for him'"
(Genesis 2:18). God intended for man and woman to be
mutually enriching to one another. He planned that husband and wife should experience a thorough sharing of
all of life together, that they should support one another and
encourage one another and talk together and walk together
and laugh and love and weep and worship — together. *Together* they were made to reflect God's image. They were
made for each other and for Him.

It is unfortunate that the full implications of this passage
are often overlooked or misunderstood. The word "help" or
"helper" is sometimes thought to mean that woman was
made as an inferior, someone to serve man, to attend to his
wishes and prepare his food and bear and care for his children. But the word thus translated is the Hebrew word
"ezer" which is used over and over in the Old Testament
in reference to *God* in such passages as "Our soul waits for
the Lord; he is our *help* and shield" (Psalm 33:20), and "I
lift up my eyes to the hills. From whence does my *help*
come? My *help* comes from the Lord, who made heaven and
earth" (Psalm 121:1, 2). The word doesn't imply that the
one who provides help is a mere servant waiting to be
beckoned and then dismissed after a duty has been performed. If Adam's need had only been for someone to run
errands and do simple "housework," etc., he could have
trained a monkey or chimpanzee for this — something recent

experiments have shown to be possible. But man's need was for a companion on the level of mind and spirit — someone with whom he could share his innermost thoughts and dreams in enriching dialogue that would uplift and enlighten.

The words translated, "fit for him" or "meet [or suitable] for him" in the original Hebrew meant literally "a help as his front," and in some translations is rendered "a help similar to him," or "a helper like unto himself." Father Lagrange, a Roman Catholic Hebrew scholar, points out that a most accurate way to put it would be "a helpmeet who is, as it were, a vis-a-vis."[7] A vis-a-vis means a person who is face to face with another — someone who is situated opposite to oneself. Thus, God gave woman to man to be his counterpart, his "other half" in a very real sense — like him in spirit, though different in body, and perfectly suited for the partnership God intended husband and wife to experience together in the presence of Him who gave them to each other.

God's plan was that husband and wife should know an intimacy that is incomparable and unparalleled. Perhaps Adam had at times looked into a pool of water, and as he pondered his reflected image, he may have yearned for one like himself. None of the animals were creatures like himself — none could meet the longing of his heart. It was, however, more than a desire for human companionship — God could easily have brought another man to Adam if his need had only been for a friend. But the sense of incompleteness Adam felt was part of the Lord's design in creating mankind in two sexes. He made man and woman to complement and supplement one another and to experience in marriage a closeness which in itself may be a reflection of God's image. (Some theologians feel that the close bond and loving fel-

---

[7]Quoted in E. Danniel and B. Olivier, *Woman is the Glory of Man*, trans. by M. Angeline Bouchard (Westminster, Md.: The Newman Press, 1964), p. 7.

lowship of a husband and wife helps us understand something of the relationship of Father, Son, and Holy Spirit.)

Thus, when God brought to Adam the wife He had made for him, Adam was filled with wonder and exclaimed, "At last! Bone of my bones and flesh of my flesh!" He realized she was, in the truest sense, a part of him; and he regarded her as his very own self. St. Paul alludes to this tender devotion in his passage comparing the husband-wife relationship to the union of Christ and His Church. "Husbands should love their wives as their own bodies. He who loves his wife loves himself. For no man ever hates his own flesh, but nourishes and cherishes it, as Christ does the church, because we are members of his body" (Ephesians 5:28-30). In Christian marriage, the husband and wife regard themselves as members or parts of each other. There is a shared imtimacy experienced together that is possible with no one else. This doesn't mean, of course, that a husband and wife have no existence apart from one another or that they must think alike on even the most trivial matters — there is the "vis-a-vis" aspect of the relationship as well as the total merging. It does mean that mutually they enhance one another, are considerate of each other, and endeavor to help one another cultivate to the full his or her potentialities in all areas; because each knows that all that concerns one partner is also of concern to the other. The husband and wife belong to one another and are incomplete apart from each other. Again, this presents a tremendous illustration in the awesome analogy: "The church is Christ's body, the completion [or complement] of Him who Himself completes all things everywhere" (Ephesians 1:23, TEV).

Marriage involves the establishment of a new social unit. Jesus pointed out that it was *God* who said, "For this reason a man shall leave his father and mother and be joined to his wife" (Matthew 19:5; Genesis 2:24). As we saw earlier in this chapter, there is a *social* side of marriage — an aspect that concerns other people — that is also part of God's plan for the sake of order in society. Thus, marriage involves taking leave of one family (father and mother) and the establishment of another family (with one's wife or husband). The couple is now recognized by others as a wedded pair, a new conjugal unit.

The word translated "cleave to" or "be joined to" means literally "to be glued together." In entering the marriage relationship according to Christ's ideal for His own, a man and woman form the closest association that can be entered — their lives are bonded or cemented together inseparably.

In the ideal set forth by Christ, marriage is a binding, lifelong union. "What therefore God has joined together, let no man put asunder" (Matthew 19:6). A statement so final and binding was met by the Pharisees' rejoinder: "Why then did Moses command one to give a certificate of divorce, and to put her away?" Jesus' reply, as Patrick Fairbairn has written, showed that Moses did not *command* divorce. This was "not a privilege to be enjoyed, or a duty to be discharged, but a permission or tolerance merely suffered to continue, because of Israel's participation in the evil of the times — their moral unfitness for a more stringent application of the proper rule."[8] Christ said, "For your hardness of heart Moses *allowed* you to divorce your wives, but from the beginning it was not so." Again, Christ directs us back to the ideal established by God when He brought the first two together to be made one.

The Fall (the entrance of sin into the world because of rebellion against the Creator), of course, had a drastic effect upon the relationship between the sexes; and no one can deny the marital unhappiness all around us. The Christian has no right to *force* this ideal (e.g., by unrealistic laws) on an unbelieving society that does not live under the rule of Christ. Nor must this ideal necessarily be viewed as a cruel legalism compelling a miserable couple to remain shackled together in utter torment under any and all circumstances.

---

[8]Patrick Fairbairn, *The Revelation of Law in Scripture* (reprint of 1869 edition) (Grand Rapids, Mich.: Zondervan Publishing House, 1957), p. 128.

No less a one than the great John Milton (who himself experienced an unhappy marriage, though never divorce) wondered if perhaps in some cases, God would not still tolerate divorce for the "hardness of men's hearts" — i.e., human fallibility — just as He had in Moses' time; and there are tragic cases of marital failure today that cause some Christians to ask the same question. At any rate, the church has no right to treat a divorced person as an outcast — love and forgiveness are still Christ's way.

But the *ideal*, the principle of indissoluble union taught by Christ, must be kept foremost in our thinking. The time to get this clearly in mind is *before marriage*, not after a hasty entrance into a relationship to which one is ill-suited. Again we must remember the power of the Risen Saviour that is available to every Christian. When mankind disobeyed God, the image of God in man became marred so that only a *dim* reflection remained of what God planned man to be. But in Jesus Christ, that image is restored (Colossians 3:10). In daily newness of life, the redeemed couple *can* experience this Paradise ideal of marriage that was the Creator's design. It was *God* who brought the first husband and wife together; and He is just as interested today in bringing the committed, submitted, Christian man or woman to the life-partner that He has chosen.

The sexual union is an important part of this permanent relationship of oneness. Jesus reminded His hearers of the entirety of Genesis 2:24 — "Therefore a man leaves his father and his mother and cleaves to his wife, *and they become one flesh*." That this being "one flesh" refers not only to a total overall union of personalities, but also has particular reference to the *sexual* union of husband and wife, is made clear from the Apostle Paul's statement about this in warning against coitus outside marriage (I Corinthians 6:16).

First, the Scriptures make clear that this physical joining is not an isolated *act*, but a part of a total relationship. That it is to take place *after* the marriage has been entered — after the new social unit has been formed — may be seen in the sequence of the Genesis pattern that Christ quotes (leave, cleave, become one flesh). Sexual intercourse becomes a unique way of marking the transition into that new status conferred by marriage.

Second, the Scriptures never play down the fact that the sexual side of marriage is tremendously important and intended by God to be thoroughly enjoyable for both husband and wife. This is seen, for example, in passages such as Proverbs 5:18, 19 and I Corinthians 7:3-5.

In recent years, increasing numbers of Bible scholars have been impressed that God chose to devote an entire book of the Bible to the exaltation of married love — The Song of Solomon (sometimes called The Song of Songs or Canticles). They do not view the erotic symbolism of the book as a cause for embarrassment or apology, but rather as an indication of how *God* regards sex in wedlock — that He made it to be something beautiful and pure and good. But throughout the ages, puzzled theologians (who seemed unable to see sex in this light and apparently found it difficult to believe that God could either!) came up with all sorts of explanations for the book's inclusion in the Scriptures. The favorite interpretation inferred that it had nothing at all to do with human love but was intended solely as an allegory of God's dealings with Israel or of Christ with His Church (or with the soul of the believer) and therefore referred only to a mystical, *spiritual* love.

A position gaining favor among Christians today who are seeking to learn God's will in regard to marriage is that God *intended* The Song of Solomon to portray love as He planned it for husband and wife. Speaking of this, Meredith G. Kline has written:

> This view, though only in modern times enjoying ecclesiastical respectability, can be traced as far back as the evidence for the history of interpretation goes. And why should the Church stumble at the presence in her inspired canon of a song extolling the dignity and beauty of human love and marriage? Considering how large the subject looms in the attention of men, had it not been remarkable

if there were not such an extended treatment of it in the volume God has given us for "reproof, for correction, for instruction in righteousness"? And all the more so when we think how sordid is the world's attitude towards the matter and how dim had become even the Old Testament saint's apprehension of the paradisaic ideal of marriage. . . . The Song confronts us with love as it was in the beginning and it lets us hear again the divine marriage benediction first addressed to the lover and his beloved in man's home primeval (Genesis 1:28a). What the incarnate Word did for the sanctity of marriage by His presence at the Cana wedding, the written Word does by dwelling with joy upon conjugal love in the Song of Songs.[9]

Many years earlier, John Richard Sampey sounded a similar note in *The International Standard Bible Encyclopedia*:

Even if Canticles is merely a collection of songs describing the bliss of true lovers in wedlock, it is not thereby rendered unworthy of a place in the Bible, unless marriage is to be regarded as a fall from a state of innocency. . . . Perhaps most persons need to enlarge their conception of the Bible as a repository for all things that minister to the welfare of men. The entire range of man's legitimate joys finds sympathetic and appreciative description in the Bible. Two young lovers in Paradise need not fear to rise and meet their Creator, should He visit them in the cool of the day.[10]

This view of the Song of Songs (sometimes called the literal or "natural" view) doesn't mean, of course, that one cannot also find therein rich devotional material (for example, the hymn, "Loved with Everlasting Love" is based on

---

[9]Meredith G. Kline, "The Song of Songs," *Christianity Today*, April 27, 1959, p. 39. Reprinted by permission.

[10]John Richard Sampey, "Song of Songs," in *The International Standard Bible Encyclopedia*, James Orr, Ed., Vol. V. (Grand Rapids, Mich.: Wm. B. Eerdmans Publishing Co., 1939), pp. 2833-4. Used by permission.

this book), nor that it cannot portray the close relationship between Christ and His Church or depict the love of God. We have already seen that the ideal of marriage *is* to serve as a picture of God's covenant relationship with His people. And if Canticles helps us better understand marriage, it can indeed help us understand more of the believer's union and communion with his Lord.

Primarily, however, it has much to teach us about wedded love as God intended it to be. One cannot help but be impressed by the lovers' *utter delight in one another*. All through the book it is made clear that this man and this woman enjoy each other totally. They long to be together and miss one another dreadfully when apart. This comes through clearly in the reverie of the bride-to-be in the first three chapters. There she recalls moments with her beloved and daydreams about their future together. She remembers their conversations and endearments spoken. Occasionally, she expresses a secret fear of losing him; but even as the thought crosses her mind, her eyes are straining to catch his coming in the distance. She knows he *will* come for her: he is hers and she is his. After the wedding (she is addressed as a bride beginning with chapter 4), she has a nightmare that she has turned her beloved away, and again she acknowledges her great need for his love. To be forsaken by him would be the most terrible catastrophe that could ever befall her (5:2 ff.).

The man and woman who are the subjects of this love-poem have a desire for one another exclusively. This is not an infatuation based on physical longing; each sees the other as a *person* — not as a shapely form or handsome body only. Each is persuaded that no one can compare with the beloved. The man tells the one he loves that she is a lovely flower, and compared to her, all other girls are just thorns. She replies that he is a luxuriant apple tree — teeming with sweet fruit and providing cool, restful shade. In comparison to him, she says, all other young men are common trees of wood. When anyone asks, "What is your beloved more

than any other beloved?" the young woman can scarcely
contain her praise for him.

Throughout the book, there is an insistence that love is
something very serious — not something to be toyed and
trifled with. It must not be artificially and prematurely
whipped up. The young woman warns her girl friends of the
foolishness of awaking love "until it please" (2:7; 3:5). It is
not something to be stirred up by sexually stimulating situations and conduct that would incite sheer physical passion.
Time must be allowed for a lasting, loving relationship to
develop. Real love will awaken at the *right* time — will bud
and blossom and bloom in all its fullness as a man and
woman grow together and learn to know each other, thereby
reaching the point of deciding to make a total commitment
to one another for life. One doesn't fall in and out of this
kind of love.

This does not mean, of course, that in the gradual development of such a relationship there will be no physical
desire. Such desire comes as an outgrowth of an inner love
longing to be expressed toward this very special one. But
because the physical expression of affection is viewed in the
context of the total relationship and all that it means, the
couple is able to exercise self-control and avoid being carried away in a manner that would be regretted later. Yet,
both lovers are open and candid about their feelings. The
young woman speaks of yearning for his kisses at the very
beginning of the song and as she dreams of her husband-
to-be, she admits to a very literal case of lovesickness and
longs for his embraces (2:5, 6). The young man apparently
experiences similar feelings, and on their honeymoon tells
his wife, "You have ravished my heart, my sister, my bride,
you have ravished my heart with a glance of your eyes"
(4:9). At one point, he finds it necessary to say, "Don't look
at me that way!" He asks her to turn away her eyes from
him because he is overwhelmed by the love shining from
them (6:5).

Before the wedding, there is, however, real restraint in
the degree of physical intimacy permitted. Looking back on

those days, the bride recalls the necessity of avoiding the show of affection in public — which would have been considered indecent. She confesses that there were times she had found herself wishing her fiance were one of her brothers so that she could run outside and greet him with kisses (8:1, 2). But she has no regrets for the premarital reserve she and her betrothed had practiced. After the wedding (perhaps during the days of feasting and celebration), the family discusses her little sister's future, wondering what she will be like as she develops into young maidenhood and experiences the attention of boys. Will she be a wall or a door? Reserved with the opposite sex? Or permitting such free access that she'll need guarding by the family? (Perhaps this is a recollection of a conversation referring to the bride herself as a child.)

The young bride looks back on her own life and is glad that she was a "wall." No one had to guard her; she was able to "keep [her] heart with all vigilance, for from it flow the springs of life" (Proverbs 4:23). She had a goal in mind — the goal of one day being able to give herself wholly and solely to her marriage partner (4:12, 16; 5:1). And because of this, she was "in his eyes as one who brings peace" — a source of comfort, solace, warmth and joy (8:8-10).

Incidentally, virginity, viewed this way, is not looked upon as a mere sign of "respectability" and bowing to society's conventions, nor as a symptom of inhibitions based on a low view of sex, nor as an emblem of "victory" over all the forces undertaking to "rob" one's person and bring about an irreplaceable loss, nor as an indication that one "never had the opportunity" for coitus (according to the Kinsey report, 22 percent of virginal females and more than a third of virginal males "blamed" their chastity on "lack of opportunity"![11]) Rather, the Biblical ideal of chastity for both men and women indicates that virginity should be viewed as a *positive value* to be brought to the marriage —

---

[11]Reiss, *op. cit.,* p. 196n.

a symbol of the uniqueness of the marriage relationship. The husband and wife are presenting each other with a gift that is a token of their total self-giving. They are reciprocally granting access to a part of themselves that no one else has ever shared. There is nothing *negative* about chastity from this point of view. The stress is not on self-denial and "abstaining from," but rather on "saving for" and "bringing to" marriage this unique bestowal that involves both giver and recipient at the deepest level of their beings. For every person who ever engages in coitus, there is, of course, a *first* sexual union. When a husband and wife experience that first union *with each other*, the "one flesh" relationship is marked in a very special way. And this is God's plan.

Contrary to a popular modern notion that sexual adjustment on the wedding night will be more difficult if premarital sex has not been engaged in, this young bride and bridegroom do not find their first sexual intercourse in any way distasteful or difficult because of shame or fear or tensions or inhibitions. Rather, they both experience sheer delight (e.g., 4:1—5:1). Their great love, their high view of sex, and their mutual attitude of anticipation is what makes the difference. They are joyful that at last the moment has come when their immense love can be poured into one another in the closest embrace possible. There is uninhibited freedom and absolute abandonment as they express that love in caresses and kisses and the union of bodies. And such creativity, delight, and vitality in the sexual expression of love can grow and become even more pleasurable over the years as their love continues to grow.

The language describing these most intimate, personal aspects of holy wedlock is neither prudish nor even remotely offensive or obscene. With restraint and delicacy, through poetic symbolism, the marriage bed is portrayed in terms of all that is lovely and beautiful and pure — fragrant spices and flowering gardens, fountains and streams, milk and honey, and fruits and wine, ivory and precious jewels, the singing of birds, and graceful animals racing and romping over the hills. This is the picture of wedded love that God has given as part of His Word to us. As an expression of the complete commitment of a man and woman to one another, sexual intercourse can be looked upon as something for which to give thanks to the Lord. How wonderful that He designed such a marvelous way for a husband and wife to be fused together so that very literally they *do* become one!

The basic attitude of this couple in accepting their love (and the privilege of expressing it sexually) as a wonderful gift of God enables them to appreciate and adore one another's bodies as flawless exhibits of His handiwork. There is no embarrassment or shame between the spouses in viewing the human form. Both the muscular firmness of the male physique and the soft contours of the female figure are seen as objects of beauty and ceaseless wonder (e.g., 4:1 ff.; 5:10-16; 6:4—7:9).

Before leaving the Song of Solomon, it should be pointed out that the greater portion of this book is taken up with the *woman's* thoughts on love. From God's point of view, there is nothing indecent or indecorous in a woman's active participation in and enjoyment of sexual relations with her husband — contrary to Victorian notions which are still occasionally propagated in Christian circles today. The Christian wife has no reason to feel ashamed or guilty about the sexual urge she knows to be a part of her. God planned for her to be a creative participant, a sharer and co-partner with her husband in their sexual union — not a passive, unimaginative submissive "object" who is acted *upon* instead of a person acting *with*.

The Song of Songs is a poem of love in which the lovers cannot get over their sense of wonder at belonging to each other (e.g., 2:16; 6:3; 7:10). There is an intensity, a fervency, and enduring strength in their love. Such love is like a flaming fire that not even surging floodwaters could extinguish. And all the money in the world could never buy love like this (8:6, 7). This is the model of marriage that God has given us.

Parenthood is a privilege that is part of the marriage relationship. The Genesis account of the origin of marriage speaks of God's blessing on the first husband and wife and His admonition to be fruitful and multiply. The Bible does not insist that the begetting of offspring is the main purpose of sex, but it does make clear that children are "an heritage of the Lord" (Psalm 127:3). The experience of bearing and rearing children together and training them in the ways of God (Deuteronomy 6:4-7) is a priceless privilege that enhances the partnership of a husband and wife.

God directs some to a life of singleness. When Jesus' disciples heard His comments on marriage in Matthew 19, they brought up the matter of singleness. Christ acknowledged that there were some who were single through no fault of their own, but there were others who accepted a life of singleness for the sake of the kingdom of God. Such people are willing to delay marriage or even to forego it altogether because of demands required of them in serving God. In our day, it might be true of certain types of missionary work, or where a man desires to live in some area of the inner city in order to fully identify with the people and be free to carry on a ministry with street gangs or drug addicts or others with special needs. It might be true of a woman whose ministry requires much travel and a flexibility of schedule that would be difficult if not impossible if she had a husband and children.

But both Christ and Paul made clear that singleness is only for a certain few for whom God wills it (either temporarily or permanently). Every follower of Christ should be willing to accept the possibility that this may be what God wants for him or her, knowing all the while, however, that God will supply the strength, comfort, and power to live a rich, full life even without the experience of marriage. But for most, marriage will likely be the way of life to which God directs. It is probable that even the disciples who had asked Jesus about singleness (after their initial shock at realizing the demands intrinsic in the marriage ideal Christ set forth) eventually found wives whom they regarded as gifts from God (I Corinthians 9:5; Proverbs 18:22; 19:14).

In this chapter, we have viewed marriage both sociologically and theologically, with the hope that a clearer understanding of the nature and purpose of marriage may aid in clarifying thoughts about the place of sex in man-woman relationships. Again, it must be emphasized that sex and marriage are not man-woman affairs alone, but are concerns of man, woman, God, and society.

8

The Single Eye

Throughout the Scriptures, from the thunderings of Sinai to the celestial visions at Patmos, God makes it clear that He will not put up with idolatry. He tells us that He is a jealous God who demands exclusive possession of His redeemed ones (Exodus 20:1-5; Deuteronomy 4:23, 24; 11:16). He insists on our *total* allegiance. "I am the Lord, that is my name; my glory I give to no other, nor my praise to graven images" (Isaiah 42:8).

The same message continues to come through in the New Testament and is perhaps summed up most succinctly in the Apostle John's admonition: "Little children, keep yourselves from idols" (I John 5:21). Jesus showed that no man can have two masters (two gods); to love one means hating the other and vice versa (Matthew 6:24). Full attention to God leaves no room for undivided loyalty to any other pursuit, person, or possession that likewise calls for absolute homage.

In *The Cost of Discipleship*, Dietrich Bonhoeffer pointed out that it was no accident that fornication and covetousness are so often mentioned side by side in New Testament lists of vices, and that both are designated as idolatry.[1] Sex, like money, can become a person's god ever so easily —

---

[1]Dietrich Bonhoeffer, *The Cost of Discipleship* (New York: Macmillan Paperbacks Edition, 1963), p. 194.

often without one's even being aware of what is happening. It is no coincidence that sexual promiscuity and idolatry have been so closely linked throughout history. Cult prostitutes, phallic images, and ritual orgies were all part of the ceremonial worship of pagan divinities which the Lord God detested. The Apostle Paul says that the punishment meted out to Israel for its participation in such rites should serve as a warning to Christian believers today (I Corinthians 10:6-14).

This linkage between casual sex and *idolatry* may shed some further light on a clarification of Christian sexual ethics. The reason is twofold: First, as has already been mentioned, sex itself can be an idol. Second, if the marriage relationship is analogous to the relationship between God and His people (a figure used repeatedly in both Old and New Testaments), then promiscuity is definitely ruled out. As Harold O. J. Brown has expressed it:

> The main problem behind promiscuity, the factor which explains why God requires monogamy and faithfulness, is that sexual license teaches man to misunderstand the nature of love and the fact that God desires to train our affections here for a single, faithful, unitary relationship to Him. This is undoubtedly the reason why idolatry in the Old Testament is so often referred to as adultery.[2]

The Bible frequently uses terms such as "played the harlot with other gods" to depict the unfaithfulness of God's people in turning away from Him and yielding devotion to idols. "Surely, as a faithless wife leaves her husband, so have you been faithless to me, O house of Israel, says the Lord" (Jeremiah 3:20). "You have played the harlot with many lovers; and would you return to me? says the Lord. Lift up your eyes to the bare heights and see! Where have you not been lain with?" (Jeremiah 3:1b-2a). "You have played the harlot, forsaking your God" (Hosea 9:1). "I will punish

---

[2]Harold O. J. Brown, "The College Student Today," *Eternity*, June, 1965, p. 18. Reprinted by permission.

her for the feast days of the Baals when she burned incense to them and decked herself with her ring and jewelry, and went after her lovers, and forgot me, says the Lord" (Hosea 2:13).

Some of the most frank, vivid descriptions in which casual, promiscuous sex symbolizes spiritual unfaithfulness are found in the book of Ezekiel (e.g., chapters 16, 20, 23). In Ezekiel 23, the two kingdoms of divided Israel are portrayed as two sisters who delighted in sexual looseness. "They played the harlot in Egypt; they played the harlot in their youth; there their breasts were pressed and their virgin bosoms handled" (v. 3). Even the marriage relationship failed to change them. God says:

> Oholah [Northern Kingdom] played the harlot while she was mine; and she doted on her lovers. . . . She bestowed her harlotries upon them . . . and she defiled herself with all the idols of every one on whom she doted. She did not give up her harlotry which she had practiced since her days in Egypt; for in her youth men had lain with her and handled her virgin bosom and poured out their lust upon her. Therefore I delivered her into the hands of her lovers, into the hands of the Assyrians, upon whom she doted . . . she became a byword among women, when judgment had been executed upon her. (Ezekiel 23:5-10)

A warning of similar judgment was issed to the other kingdom, because her spiritual adultery was no different.

The exclusiveness and uniqueness of the marriage relationship, in which a man and woman give themselves sexually to one another only (as a unifying bond signifying their belonging to one another in every other way as well) obviously rules out casual, hedonistic sex with other people — both before and after marriage. To ignore or flout this idea of exclusiveness is abhorrent to God — if for no other reason than that the institution of marriage is a means of helping mankind catch some small glimpse of the singular devotion and undivided loyalty God requires of those who enter into a covenant relationship with Him. Alluding to the Hebrew wedding custom of spreading a skirt or garment over the bride to symbolize her belonging to her husband, God said to Israel, ". . . You were at the age for love; and I spread my skirt over you . . . yea, I plighted my troth to you and entered into a covenant with you . . . and you became mine" (Ezekiel 16:8). Other references related to the subject of marriage as an illustration of God's relationship to believers are Isaiah 54:5; 61; 62; Jeremiah 2:2; Hosea 2:14-23 (cf. Romans 9:25; Hebrews 10:16, 17; I Peter 2:9, 10); Ephesians 3:11-13; 5:25-32; Mark 2:19; John 3:29; Revelation 19:7 ff.

"I am jealous for you, with a divine jealousy," wrote Paul to the Corinthian Christians, "for I betrothed you as a chaste virgin to her true and only husband. But as the serpent in his cunning seduced Eve, I am afraid that your thoughts may be corrupted and you may lose your singlehearted devotion to Christ" (II Corinthians 11:2, 3, NEB). The singlehearted devotion of a husband and wife who have reserved the sexual expression of love for marriage, who know they have shared their bodies with no one but each other, and who are pledged to be faithful to one another always, provides us with a picture of the singleness of mind and heart that God requires in the Christian's relationship to Him. The Divine Lover wants the believer to belong to Him alone — to be His completely — to be His forever. This means the Christian must determine to experience the single eye — a gaze which turns away from the disappointing mirages of happiness proffered by the world and instead fastens upon the One who loved His bride enough to give His all in order to make her His own (Ephesians 5).

> The bride eyes not her garment,
>   But her dear bridegroom's face;
> I will not gaze at glory,
>   But on my King of grace.[3]

---

[3]From the hymn, "The Sands of Time Are Sinking" by Anne R. Cousin, 1857.

This is the single eye. Its vision is limited to Jesus Christ, leaving no room for idols of any sort — no matter how dazzling they may seem.

"But," someone says at this point, "this doesn't apply to my girl and me. We can understand that Christ wants our wholehearted devotion and that this means idolatry is definitely *out*. And we can see that sex itself *could* become an idol for many people, so that they find themselves living for the pleasures of the body — lusting and longing and forgetting all about God.

"And we agree that God's relationship to His people is all-demanding and can see how this must be reflected in a faithful, exclusive relationship between one man and one woman who give themselves totally to one another and to no one else.

"But here's our problem: None of this applies to our personal situation! My fiancee and I love each other deeply and we'd like to express that love to the full — in an uninhibited way. In other words, we have a strong desire to go to bed together. We've pledged ourselves to each other only — so it wouldn't be a case of promiscuity, would it? We'd still be fulfilling the picture of exclusive devotion to 'the one and only,' just as in an actual marriage relationship. We don't feel sex would become an idol to us. Why should sex be considered idolatrous for an engaged couple any more than it would be for a married couple?"

Since this type of argument is not infrequently heard these days among Christian young adults, it deserves comment.

First, it would seem that one reason God has ordained that His good gift of sex be placed *within the institution of marriage* is that it is much less likely to become an idol in this context. Why? Because marriage is so much more than sex.

The very idea of marriage involves *reciprocal obligations* on the part of both partners. Publicly, a man and woman enter into a legal contract entailing mutual rights and responsibilities. Sexual gratification is not "something for nothing" in the marriage relationship, but is intertwined with obligations to one's spouse, one's future children, and one's society — as we saw earlier. In contrast, outside marriage, sexual pleasure is sought without being bound up with any such obligations and responsibilities. No binding agreement exists to keep in check any tendencies to act selfishly, to exploit, to take advantage of someone for personal ends. There is not the security of marriage to stabilize the relationship with the confidence that faithfulness and permanence are required and expected. Engagements can be and often are broken; and the greater the sexual intimacy has been, the greater the likelihood that the hurt of breaking up will be deep indeed.

For reasons such as these, sex is far more likely to become an idol to couples outside matrimony than it is to a wedded pair. To the unmarried couple engaging in sexual intercourse, it is not at all uncommon for sex to become the *main focus* of their relationship. "All week long I find myself just living for the weekend when we can hop into bed together." "We're finding that our whole relationship centers more and more around our sex experience these days." "Since we've begun having regular sex relations, we're finding our communication in other areas is breaking down. When we're together, we don't talk much any more — we take for granted our time together will be spent in sex. Somehow, though, I feel we're missing something — that we're not relating to each other as persons lately, just bodies." These are typical statements of couples who have decided to go ahead with premarital sexual relations. The danger of idolatry should be obvious to any thinking Christian.

In contrast, sexual idolatry would seem to be much less likely to occur within marriage because of the very nature of marriage. There sex relations are a normal part of a way of life — not some flaming event isolated from all the other rights, pleasures, and responsibilities of the shared life of husband and wife. Economic interdependence, the mutual privileges and duties of parenthood, household tasks and obligations, and functioning as a socially recognized family unit in the community are just as much a part of the "one flesh" relationship as is sexual intercourse. Sex is far more likely to be viewed in perspective when it is thus seen as only *one* part of an overall relationship — and a *demanding* relationship at that.

Someone has pointed out that throughout the ages there has been a tendency to worship sex as "the ultimate divinity." Perhaps one reason God instituted marriage was to provide a way for the marvelous ecstasies of sex to be experienced to the full, but in a context where built-in safeguards lessen the probability of idolatry.

A second and equally crucial issue must be raised in regard to the Christian engaged couple. This has to do with the matter of *obedience to God*. If God has revealed His will to be that sexual intercourse must be reserved for marriage, then to disobey Him is another form of idolatry — the setting up of the graven image of self-will.

Only in recent years have questions been raised about the explicitness and clarity of the Bible's statements in regard to premarital sex. Among the main reasons for this questioning have been (1) the current contention that the Ten Commandments are silent about premarital sex and that the adultery commandment had nothing to do with sex *per se* but was concerned only with a husband's property rights (see discussion on this in Chapter 6), (2) the allegation that the Greek word for fornication didn't refer to couples in love, but warned only against having sexual relations with a prostitute or in a promiscuous fashion, and (3) the emphasis on affection and a meaningful, stable relationship as the factors which decide the legitimacy of sexual intercourse, rather than whether or not it occurs within the wedded state.

All three of these arguments have been discussed to a certain degree earlier in this book, but perhaps the matter should be faced head-on at this point. Are the new moralists incorrect? *Does* the Bible make clear that premarital sexual intercourse is contrary to the will of God? A close examination of all relevant Scripture indicates that the answer is *yes* — that obedience to God requires the believer to reserve coitus for marriage.

Why is this? And how can a Christian know for sure that premarital chastity is God's will? There are at least seven arguments leading to this conclusion, and each will be examined briefly. (Parts of the following discussion may at points seem repetitious in view of earlier chapters, but are reviewed here in an effort to present a summary of Biblical teaching on the why of chastity.)

1. Christ's Teaching on Marriage.

In Matthew 19:3 ff., Jesus Christ showed that marriage for a Christian couple involves (1) *a change in social status* — and usually in place of residence ("For this reason a man shall leave his father and mother"), (2) *the establishment of a new relationship* — a new social unit — involving a unique bond ("and be joined [cleave] to his wife"), and (3) *sexual intercourse* as a sign and seal of that bond of oneness ("and the two shall become one flesh" — one body). All three aspects of the relationship are acknowledged to be part of a *lifelong partnership* — a union in which *God* has joined the believing husband and wife together as one unit. The expression of love through the "one flesh" relationship (sexual intercourse) *follows* the "leaving" and the "cleaving" — it does not precede it. Becoming physically "one flesh" presupposes a socially recognized and legitimate marriage relationship — a commitment entered with the intention and expectation of permanence. This, Jesus indicated, was the Creator's plan from the beginning.

2. Christ's Teaching on the Seventh Commandment.

Christ never revoked the commandment, "You shall not commit adultery," nor did He ever indicate that such a specific command was no longer necessary in view of a higher law of Christian love. Rather, He quoted the commandment (Matthew 19:18), alluded to it (Mark 7:21), and extended it (Matthew 5:27, 28). He gave no hint that

God's issuance of a special command about adultery had anything to do with the mere violation of another man's exclusive rights to the sexual possession of his wife. (If that were the case, there would have been no need for such a specific command. The situation would have been covered in the commandments forbidding covetousness and stealing.)

When Jesus said, "If a man looks on a woman with a lustful eye, he has already committed adultery with her in his heart" (Matthew 5:28 NEB), He was speaking of sin against God — not an offense against one's neighbor in this instance. In this particular case, no other person is outwardly or actively involved — except in the *thought-life* of someone else. There is no indication of a husband's actual awareness of another man's lewd desires for his wife; and in all probability the woman looked upon hasn't the remotest notion that a masculine acquaintance is imagining himself in bed with her! Thus, although no other person is actually harmed, the commission of sin has nonetheless occurred — even though it has taken place only in one's mind.

Jesus called *hatred* murder (Matthew 5:21ff.), as did the Apostle John (I John 3:15), and this is breaking the sixth commandment even though no blood has been shed. The Christian cannot — must not — overlook his responsibility to God and the necessity of obeying the moral law He has given. "For whoever keeps the whole law but fails in one point has become guilty of all of it. For he who said, 'Do not commit adultery,' said also, 'Do not kill.' If you do not commit adultery but do kill, you have become a transgressor of the law" (James 2:10, 11).

Man looks on the outward appearance, but God sees the heart. "There is nothing that can be hid from God. Everything in all creation is exposed and lies open before His eyes; and it is to Him that we must all give account of ourselves" (Hebrews 4:13 TEV). Thus, Jesus showed that even the sensual *longing* to have sexual relations with someone other than one's spouse is a breaking of God's commandment. As we saw in Chapter 6, Christ's teaching made clear that this is not intended for married people only, but likewise should be applied to the single person and to the matter of pre-marital sexual behavior and attitudes.

3. The Bible's Warnings Against Committing Fornication.

Exponents of the new morality do not believe that the Greek word *porneia* (usually translated "fornication" or "immorality" in the Bible) can be applied to premarital sex when practiced by a mutually consenting man and woman within a stable love relationship. They feel that "fornication" refers to the idea of depersonalized, body-centered sex that does not take into account the human personality of the partner, maintaining that it has special reference to consorting with a prostitute (as indeed it does in I Corinthians 6:15, 16) and to casual, indiscriminate promiscuous sex.

No reputable Bible scholar would deny that *porneia* did include such meanings, but there is widespread disagreement about limiting the word to these meanings alone. There is a great deal of evidence on the side of those who insist that "in the New Testament the words for 'fornication,' 'to practice fornication,' etc. refer to every kind of sexual intercourse outside marriage."[4] Professor E. M. Blaiklock of the University of Auckland, New Zealand, who is internationally known as a classical scholar, points out that the word was often used with reference to the nature-cults, "a not remote parallel to the sentimentalised promiscuity condoned by some of the exponents of the new morality." "You can be sure," he says, "that in New Testament contexts no writer would think of the word in other than a pejorative context, including under its meaning all sex-experience outside the

---

[4]O. J. Baab, "Fornication," *The Interpreter's Dictionary of the Bible* (New York and Nashville: Abingdon Press, 1962). Used by permission. Also see articles on fornication in *The Zondervan Pictorial Bible Dictionary* (Zondervan, 1963), *Baker's Dictionary of Theology* (Baker, 1960), *The New Smith's Bible Dictionary* (Doubleday, 1966), *Harper's Bible Dictionary* (Harper, 1954), *New Catholic Encyclopedia* (McGraw-Hill, 1967), as well as Bible commentaries from various theological viewpoints in their exegesis on passages containing *porneia* (e.g. *The Interpreter's Bible*, Abingdon, 1955).

one legitimate occasion — marriage. . . . There is not a phrase or word in the New Testament which in any way condones extra-marital sex. . . . The whole force of the New Testament is behind chastity and the sanctity of marriage."[5]

This was the meaning that came through clearly to Christians of New Testament times and is why the command to "flee fornication" was repeated so often. It was such a *new* idea to converts from paganism (who did not even have the high moral background of Judaism to draw upon but had been accustomed to regard sexual looseness as the normal state of affairs for mankind). Yet, as the Thessalonian Christians were instructed, God's purpose was a holiness that "entails first of all a clean cut with sexual immorality" (I Thessalonians 4:3, Phillips). Paul goes on to state that this is not merely his personal opinion, but a command of God, and that anyone who regards it lightly is flouting not man's rules, but God's (I Thessalonians 4:8). "Let marriage be held in honor among all, and let the marriage bed be undefiled; for God will judge the immoral [fornicators] and adulterous" (Hebrews 13:4).

4. *Arguments from Inference.*

The brief article on sex in *The Standard Jewish Encyclopedia* shows that in Judaism, "all intimacy outside marriage is illicit." The article states that "while recognizing the normality of the sexual appetite, Jewish law insists that it should find satisfaction within the marriage bond and makes extensive provision for its regulation and control."[6]

No one can deny that there existed sexual abuses in abundance during Bible times (the Bible never hides this fact), just as there are abuses of sex today. But a close examination of the customs of the people of God in both

---

[5]E. M. Blaiklock, in a letter to the author, January 17, 1968. Quoted by permission.

[6]Cecil Roth, Editor in Chief, *The Standard Jewish Encyclopedia,* Revised Third Ed. (Garden City, N.Y.: Doubleday and Company, Inc., 1966). Quoted by permission.

Old and New Testaments clearly indicates that *chastity before marriage* and *faithfulness within marriage* were the norms. The great stress on virginity for Israelite maidens, culminating in formal examinations to prove the bride's virginity as part of the marriage ceremonies (a social — not a private — concern), obviously makes it clear that godly women of Bible times would not consider it "right" or "proper" to engage in premarital sexual relations. That this was also the norm for men (if not always the actual practice) may be inferred from the fact that men were specifically commanded, under punishment of death, not to commit adultery with another man's wife or betrothed; and they were likewise warned of the evil of consorting with harlots. If a man had sexual relations with an unmarried and unbetrothed girl, he had to pay a high bride price and marry her to make up for the disgrace he had brought upon her. These rules and their penalties obviously placed great restrictions on a man's opportunities for premarital sexual intercourse, and it must have been clear that a man as well as a woman was to reserve coitus for marriage. If prostitutes, married women, engaged women, and unattached women were out of bounds, who was left as a possible premarital partner? The girl he loved? No, because to have intercourse with his betrothed in advance of the wedding would bring great social disgrace in view of all the stress on a bride's virginity. It seems to have been implicitly understood that chastity before marriage was the standard to which both men and women were expected to comply (cf. Isaiah 62:5).

In various Scripture references, the figures of fountains, streams, and cisterns euphemistically refer to the sexual powers, energies, organs, and appetites of both men and women. That one should "drink" only within the marriage relationship is made clear (even though tempting voices may claim that "stolen water is sweet" [Proverbs 9:16, 17]). Thus, a man is told in Proverbs 5:15-19: "Drink water from your own cistern, flowing water from your own well. Should your springs be scattered abroad, streams of water in the streets?"

[This would be applicable to a single man as well as to a married man.] "Let them be for yourself alone, and not for strangers with you. Let your fountain be blessed and rejoice with the wife of your youth, a lovely hind, a graceful doe. Let her affection fill you at all times with delight, be infatuated (lit. 'intoxicated') with her love." The passage goes on to stress the importance of self-discipline and to point out that a man must give an account to God for misuse of the sexual drive, "for a man's ways are before the eyes of the Lord."

The same figures are used to symbolize sex from a woman's point of view in a beautiful passage from the Song of Solomon (Song of Solomon 4:10—5:1). Here the bride invites her beloved husband to "enter the garden" which has been reserved for him alone. His admiration and delight in his new wife includes his description of her as a locked or barred garden, a spring or cistern that is shut up, and a fountain sealed. In Bible lands, gardens were locked for the sake of privacy, and outlets of water supply sources (such as fountains and cisterns) were sealed off to conserve water.[7] Thus, this passage seems to be a clear reference to the bride's virginity.

The various "arguments from inference" cited are but a few to serve as examples which indicate the Biblical ideal to be that sex belongs in marriage.

5. The Bible's Condemnation of Promiscuity.

The Word of God is very explicit in stating that promiscuity (sexual intercourse with a variety of partners) is sin against God. It is an infraction of God's standard that one

---

[7]Hugh J. Schonfield, *The Song of Songs: The Immortal Marriage Song of Love* (London, England: Elek Books Limited, 1960), p. 92. This book contains interesting background material on the Song of Solomon as well as a new translation and interpretation of the book. A paperback edition, published by Mentor books, is now available in the United States.

man and one woman are to be made "one flesh" with one another only.

The belief that sexual relations are justified in the unmarried when an affectionate relationship is present has many shortcomings — not least of which is the very real risk of "serial" promiscuity. That is, although a girl and boy may feel they are sufficiently "in love" to permit sexual intimacy and are determined to be loyal to one another as long as these feelings of affection last (which means sexual favors will be granted to no one else during that time), they know they are *not* bound to one another only and always. There is nothing to prevent the changing of partners because of the changing of feelings. Thus, it isn't unusual for a young man or woman to move through one affair after another, desperately seeking a deep, lasting love and meaningful relationship which somehow seems elusive despite the fervency of the seeker. Besides the fact that a preoccupation with sex has the danger of hindering the development of other aspects of a relationship, hopping into bed with a procession of partners is nothing short of *promiscuity* — whether or not one is "in love" and "loyal" to each in succession.

Infatuation, passion, and fleeting feelings can so easily be mistaken for love — particularly when one's idea of love is "romantic love" which, according to popular folklore, is thought to be something over which one has no control (one "falls" into it) and which can be diagnosed only by such symptoms as the tingling sensations it produces in one thus afflicted. In a *Saturday Review* column, Jerome Beatty, Jr. reported the phone conversation of a teenage girl who told a friend that she felt sure it was the "real thing" this time because she had experienced such feelings so often in the past that she couldn't be mistaken![8] This illustrates the risk inherent in the standard which says premarital coitus is the right of those who are in love. There is always the

---

[8]Jerome Beatty, Jr., "Trade Winds" column, *Saturday Review*, January 6, 1968, p. 18.

possibility that what was thought to be "the real thing this time" may turn out to be a counterfeit — that one or the other may conclude that it isn't "true love" after all and decide to slide out of the relationship, thus opening the door to promiscuity. This changing of minds and partners is obviously much easier to do outside the marriage relationship, because marriage involves the entering of a serious and binding commitment, with legal and social regulations that cannot be taken lightly. Thus (leaving aside the question of divorce), reserving coitus for marriage serves to eliminate the risk of *serial promiscuity*.

6. Sex As a Metaphor.

Earlier we saw that both Old and New Testaments speak of the marriage relationship as an illustration of God's union with His people. This is one reason that sexual intercourse is not to be used wrongly or treated casually. Becoming "one flesh" is compared to spiritual union with Christ — "He who is united to the Lord becomes one spirit with Him" (I Corinthians 6:17). The Apostle Paul speaks of the sexual congress of a husband and wife as a great mystery, something awe-inspiring, because it so wondrously symbolizes the union of Christ and His Church (Ephesians 5:31, 32). And the passage makes clear that he is speaking of a *husband-wife* sexual relationship — nothing less — to portray this unity. (The quotation of the Genesis pattern in full shows he is referring to socially recognized *marital* affinity, not a mere joining of two bodies.)

It is the entire relationship of a husband and wife, of course, that is used as a figure setting forth the bond between Christ and the believer; but the sexual aspect of marriage is given special attention and placed on a high and holy plane because of its *particular* significance as an expressive depiction of oneness.

7. Sex in Social Context.

As has already been pointed out, sexual morality cannot be regarded as a purely individual matter, but must be viewed as something that concerns society as a whole. Marriage is the Creator's design for *order* and is His provision for the proper use of human sexual powers. The many commands and customs surrounding marriage and sex in the Scriptures indicate that there was clear recognition of the social significance of such matters and of the need for regulations and controls in this area. In viewing the teaching of Scripture, no couple has any right to feel they can disregard responsibility to God and to others in the area of sexual relationships.

The seven arguments just presented are an attempt to show that the Bible clearly teaches that sexual intercourse belongs within the marriage relationship alone. Again, the reader is reminded that what is set forth is intended for the one who is committed to Jesus Christ and seeking to learn His will in order to obey it. That is why the subject has been approached from the standpoint of Scriptural teachings, rather than from utilitarian and pragmatic considerations of the effects of premarital sex on the individual or the relationship. We cannot expect — nor do we have the right — to force this sexual ethic on a non-believer. But for the person who has experienced redemption and new life in Christ, the Biblical ideal becomes not legalism (being strait-jacketed by onerous rules), but rather the paradoxical freedom of surrender to the One we love and live to please.

9

Freedom

Perhaps no wish is expressed more fervently today than the desire for personal freedom. Self-discovery and self-determination are held up by the younger generation as values that are peerless. To some, freedom is conceived of in terms of choosing for oneself, but choosing responsibly and with full consideration of the needs and rights (and *freedom*) of others. Freedom, for other individuals, is thought of in terms of getting rid of all rules and restraints that hinder self-indulgence in any form.

This second category of freedom can be enslaving. One easily becomes captive to his own self-desire and "wants what he wants when he wants it" — no matter who or what may stand in the way. When the freedom of such a person "to do his own thing" is blocked by someone else's freedom "to do *his* own thing," the reaction is childish rancor. (Witness the behavior of certain free-speech advocates who practice footstamping, shouting, and catcalls to prevent audiences from hearing opposing points of view. Or the case of an adulterous husband who became furious upon discovering that his mistress was not confining sexual relations to him alone!)

All too often the wish for *sex* freedom is really a desire for this second type of freedom — the luxury of feeling at liberty to pursue personal pleasure without having to worry about consequences, responsibilities, or feelings of guilt and remorse. (One can, of course, conceal this motive even from oneself.) A person may rationalize that the world has "come of age" and has "outgrown" the need for rules, restrictions, and restraints — indeed, that it has outgrown the need for God Himself. This wish to be free from God and from responsibility to Him is as old as the Garden of Eden. It is by no means a phenomenon of the twentieth century! The Psalmist spoke of the rebellion of people who actually make God laugh by their arrogance and blusterous contempt for His rule (Psalm 2:1-4). In the book of Jeremiah, God asks, "Why do my people say, 'We are broken loose — we are free and will roam at large; we will come no more to You?'" (Jeremiah 2:31, *The Amplified Bible*).

Those who feel no need for God's counsel, but choose to break loose and roam at large in the pastures of sex exploration and experimentation (and often, exploitation) are exercising their human right of free choice. But the freedom promised by *hedonism* can in actuality become a miserable prison over a period of time. "They promise them freedom, but are themselves slaves of corruption; for a man is the slave of whatever has mastered him" (II Peter 2:19, NEB). Obviously, *sex* becomes a master of many.

In choosing a position on sex morals by which to order their lives, large numbers of young adults utterly reject the hedonism just discussed. The freedom they desire lies within a framework of *humanism*. They, too, want to be free to deal with each situation as it arises rather than feeling constricted by rules which determine conduct beforehand. But they are uninterested in a self-centered liberty which is concerned only with one's own gratifications and pleasures. The freedom they espouse is considerate of others — of *their* rights and needs. In determining sexual conduct in a specific situation, the humanist feels his freedom to choose whether or not to engage in coitus must take into account the partner. "Will this person's growth as a human being be enhanced or hindered by such behavior? Will intercourse strengthen or weaken our personal relationship? How can love best be served?" are the questions asked instead of, "Is it wrong?"

This position was, of course, discussed in detail in Chapter 1.

Besides the hedonistic and humanistic philosophies of freedom, there is a third alternative: the Christian position. Whereas hedonism is *self*-centered, and humanism is *other*-centered, the Christian position is *Christ*-centered. This is misunderstood by many, and this misunderstanding is a prime reason that the position is held by many to be un-tenable — a nonviable option. Most people think the Chris-tian position is *rule*-centered and concentrates only on out-ward acts while ignoring motivation and inner feelings. They feel that the Christian position can be summed up in the word *don't* (period), and that this stress on abstinence is unrealistic in our modern sex-saturated society.

Thus, in this age when a young adult feels he is privileged to make his own choice from among several ethical stan-dards — just as one chooses a pair of shoes or a brand of coffee — he may flatly reject the Christian position, conclud-ing that one of the other two (or something in-between) is better suited to his personal needs. If he conceives of the Christian position as rule-centered, his decision is certainly understandable. How could he possibly expect to live up to all that Christianity requires? The answer is simple: he couldn't. No one can.

Christianity, however, is *not* a system of ethics to be auctioned in the marketplace alongside other moralities. Christianity is Jesus Christ. This means that one cannot choose "Christian ethics" or "Christian sex standards." One can only choose *Christ*. After opening one's life to Him and entering into an exciting, vital, personal relationship with the Risen Lord, these other matters fall into place. (This isn't to say, of course, that one cannot choose chastity apart from Christ. Such a choice could be made on purely human-istic grounds.)

The redemption offered by Jesus Christ promises freedom. "To proclaim release to the captives" is what Christ came into the world to do (Luke 4:18). His life, His teaching, His death for our sake, and His resurrection were all parts of

God's way of *redeeming* us — of purchasing us from slavery to sin and Satan and death. The freedom Jesus Christ gives is unparalleled. "If the Son makes you free, you will be free *indeed*" (John 8:36).

The Scriptures, however, make clear a strange paradox: All freedom involves some kind of slavery! If one is free from God, he is a slave of sin. (This doesn't necessarily mean committing gross wickedness from man's point of view, but falling short of God's standard and rebelling against Him — if only through indifference — by desiring to be one's own master). But if one is free from slavery to sin, he becomes a slave to Christ (Romans 6:15-22).

How can slavery to Christ be called freedom? Because it entails a personal relationship with the One who desires for us the very best — the most *abundant life* possible (John 10:10). This means the Christian is not encumbered by harsh inhibitions and cruel rules that are impossible to keep. Christ frees from that kind of slavery — just as He frees from helpless slavery to self-indulgence.

The Christian is one who responds to the *good news* of Jesus: "Come to me, all of you who are tired from carrying your heavy loads, and I will give you rest. Take my yoke and put it on you, and learn from me, for I am gentle and humble in spirit, and you will find rest. The yoke I will give you is easy, and the load I will put on you is light" (Matthew 11:28-30, TEV). To be yoked to Christ means one can experience a liberty unknown elsewhere. As the hymn-writer expressed it:

> Dear Lord and Master mine,
>   Thy happy servant see;
> My Conqueror, with what joy divine,
>   Thy captive clings to Thee!
>
> I love Thy yoke to wear,
>   To feel Thy gracious bands;
> Sweetly constrained by Thy care
>   And happy in Thy hands.

No bar would I remove,
  No bond would I unbind;
Within the limits of Thy love,
  Full liberty I find.
                — Thomas H. Gill, 1863

The Christian has God's gift of liberty to do and be and
say and think *anything* — except that which displeases Him.
We are not free to indulge in that to which we were formerly
in bondage. Why crawl back into a cramped, dingy, damp
cell, when Christ has flung open the prison doors and called
us out to laugh and skip and sing in a world of warmth
and sunlight and fragrant flowers and space unmeasurable?
Not that there aren't some dark valleys to pass through even
in Christ's freedom, but He is right there with us to guide us
and give us light.

Awareness of our *freedom in Christ* and of our *slavery to
Christ* has a direct bearing on sexual attitudes and conduct.
First, it means we may not use the idea of God's grace and
freedom as an excuse to condone irresponsible sexual permissiveness or any other behavior contrary to God's will
(Galatians 5:13; I Peter 2:16). Jude warned of those who
"have no real reverence for God, and they abuse His grace
as an opportunity for immorality. They will not recognize the
only Master, Jesus Christ our Lord" (v. 4, Phillips).

If Christ is our Saviour and Master, and we desire to live
lives pleasing to Him in gratitude for what He has done for
us and in response to His love for us, *how can we be sure of
what is pleasing to Him?* We must look upon the Scriptures
as God's self-disclosure to us and search out His will in all
that is of concern to us — including the matter of sex. If
we submit ourselves to Him and ask the guidance of the
Holy Spirit in discerning what God expects of us, we shall
be gloriously surprised to find that the Word of God is *not*
a confining collection of rules and restrictions designed to
choke off pleasure and make life miserable; rather, it is indeed the "law of liberty" (James 2:12)! "Where the Spirit
of the Lord is, there is freedom" (II Corinthians 3:17). The

Psalmist wrote, "I will keep thy law continually, for ever and ever; and I shall walk at liberty, for I have sought thy precepts" (Psalm 119:44, 45).

The freedom made possible by redemption also offers us Christ's *resources*. It may not be fashionable these days to speak of the superhuman dimension of Christianity — yet apart from this, there is no Christianity. The watered-down version familiar to most people today is so utterly lacking the dynamic of the first century that it bears almost no resemblance to the vitality, spontaneity, vibrancy, courage, and joy, characterizing the early church. These men and women were really *excited* about the God who became Man in order to die for their sins and make them God's children. The thrill of the Resurrection of Jesus Christ warmed their hearts and moved their hands to serve Him and their feet to spread His message. And they knew beyond all doubt that when a life is opened to Christ, He *transforms* that person! They knew, because their own lives had been changed and were continuing to be changed day by day as the Spirit of God worked within them. "For God is at work within you, helping you want to obey Him, and then helping you do what He wants" (Philippians 2:13, *Living Letters*).

This experience should be just as real to the believer today. Christ infuses a new quality of life into the one committed to Him — indeed, *He is our life* (Colossians 3:4). Daily He desires to conform us more and more to His image. Christ is with us; Christ is *in* us! The Christian can draw on the power of the Holy Spirit for wisdom in knowing God's will and for strength in carrying it out. The person who has invited Christ into his life has the promise of the Spirit's power to enable him to resist temptation. We can "walk in the Spirit" and thereby *not* feel forced to give in to all the whims and desires of our human nature. Jesus Christ promises this new life to all who desire His rule over them.

All this brings a kind of sexual freedom that is indescribable. It means freedom from shame and fear of sex (because we know the One who created sex and pronounced it *very good*). It means freedom from an obsession with sex (because to worship and serve the creature more than the Creator is idolatry). It means freedom to know what to do about sex questions and problems (because the Lord Jesus had invited His own to bring every care and problem to Him. He will guide us in the way most pleasing to Him and best for others and for ourselves.). It means freedom from slavery to sex (because He sets us at liberty from anything that would control us). It means freedom to fully *enjoy* sex according to God's plan, in His time and way, and in the realization that it is a *gift of God*.

It means freedom to resist the exploitive use of sex, such as in advertising and certain entertainments (because we can recognize this is an abuse and misuse of God's gift). It means freedom *not to conform* — no matter how wide-spread are sexual practices that are contrary to God's will (because God makes it possible for us to avoid being "squeezed into the world's mold" but instead *transforms* us by the renewing of our minds [Romans 12:1, 2]). It means freedom to be at ease in relationships with the opposite sex (because we realize that God made male and female in His image and thus the other person deserves to be treated with the dignity due all human beings. Exploitation — the use of someone for our own ends — then becomes wrong. And since a Christian knows that a man-woman relationship does not have to be sex-centered, he can feel relaxed and learn to really know a person of the opposite sex as a *friend*.).

Christ's freedom means one can experience *forgiveness*. There can be freedom from guilt and despair. Sexual transgression is not unpardonable. There's no reason for a young person to feel Christ has nothing to offer him or her because premarital sex has already been engaged in and it's too late to think of chastity. Christ has everything to offer to such a person. He offers His love and forgiveness and His power to live according to His will in days ahead. Jesus Christ offers *Himself!* He makes all things new; He restores "the years which the swarming locust has eaten" (Joel 2:25).

God forgives and forgets. And because of His grace, we can, too. (See "Postscript" at end of book for more on this subject.)

Christ's freedom means release from pressures to judge self-worth by our possession (or lack) of something the world calls "sex appeal." (We know God's standards are far different). He gives freedom from pressures that suggest we must engage in premarital sex in order to "prove" one is a man or a woman — an adult. (We know maturity involves far more than the physical ability to mate.) Christ frees us from feeling it is necessary to use sex as a status symbol, as a means of impressing one's peers.

And Christ gives freedom from feeling under pressure to rush into marriage. This is a matter of crucial importance to a girl especially, because she has been led to believe that unless she can "catch a man," she is a failure as a woman. This notion can easily cause her to feel she must give in to a boy's desire for intimate petting and/or sexual intercourse lest he look on her as "cold" and an undesirable partner for future dates, for example. The person who is committed to Christ can know freedom from such worries, because all decisions about marriage have been placed in Christ's hands and He will direct in this crucial matter as the Christian waits upon Him and desires His guidance. Thus, one can feel relaxed about the matter instead of confused, frantic, or pressured.

The redemption and resources that are ours in Christ also involve responsibilities. This means that *both* men and women must exercise responsibility in dating behavior. It is selfish, inconsiderate, and utterly irresponsible for a young man to feel that he has the *right* to be opportunistic, to endeavor to persuade a girl to "go all the way," because he feels this is a masculine prerogative — that his need for sexual release is far greater than hers and thus it's up to her to stop him if she doesn't like it. Besides the fact that some authorities are seriously questioning the idea that male sexual drives and needs are so much more urgent than those

of females (some point out that there are societies where
the women are far more sexually aggressive than the men
and therefore conclude that differences between the sexes
may be more influenced by culture than by physical dis-
tinctions),[1] there is no justification for trying to take advantage of a fellow human being in such a way. Two
Christians on a date must share the responsibility for how
that date is conducted. It is never up to the woman alone,
nor to the man alone. God holds both accountable.

If a couple sincerely want to avoid premarital coitus and
intimate petting, they should develop some sort of strategy
in advance of any tempting situation that may arise. Control depends upon their *mutual determination* not to engage
in sexual relations. Half-hearted resolutions or naive expecta-
tions that the situation will take care of itself if a time of
sexual arousal ever occurs are not realistic ways of handling
such a crucial matter.

In his book, *Young People and Sex*, Dr. Arthur H. Cain
suggests several ways of controlling sexual impulses: open
communication between dating partners about their sexual
ideals, planning, in advance, ways to prevent sexually arous-
ing situations, and determining that if such situations do
occur that every effort will be made *immediately* to effect a
change of mood or behavior.[2] Similar suggestions are listed
in Lester Kirkendall's *Premarital Intercourse and Interpersonal Relations* in a section describing the strategy worked
out by an engaged couple who, after a few instances of
yielding to their desire for sex relations, determined to forego
further intercourse until after marriage. They shortened
their time spent in physical expressions of affection (keeping
away from places where long petting sessions would be
hard to resist), spent time in more activities where they
could do things together and at the same time steer clear of

---

[1]See the discussion on this in Ira L. Reiss, *Premarital Sexual Standards in America* (New York: The Free Press, 1960), pp. 108-112.

[2]Arthur H. Cain, *Young People and Sex* (New York: John Day
Co., 1967), p. 122.

sex temptations, spent more time in group activities with other couples, and took long drives in order to be alone together, enjoying one another's companionship and conversation as they rode along, yet without the risks of petting — which, of course, ruled out prolonged periods of parking.[3] A long walk together would provide a similar situation of privacy.

Each Christian young adult must clearly think through for himself the whole matter of sex standards and behavior. And each dating couple must face this subject openly and honestly and not be afraid to discuss it together. As followers of Christ, we are not left in confusion to be helplessly tossed about by changing standards and teachings. Rather, we are instructed to be mature in Christ through His power (Colossians 1:27, 28; Ephesians 4:13-15) — to be no longer children, expecting to be bottle-fed with an easily digested formula all prepared in advance for us by those who would insist on a simplistic solution to the matter of sex morals. "For every one who lives on milk is unskilled in the word of righteousness, for he is a child. But solid food is for the mature, for those who have their faculties trained by practice to distinguish good from evil" (Hebrews 5:13, 14).

Each Christian must search out the Scriptures for himself so that indeed he may practice the discernment spoken of by the writer to the Hebrews. And this can be (and should be) made a matter of earnest prayer; God promises wisdom to those who ask.

There need be no reluctance to commit one's sex-life to God, any more than we need hesitate or fear to submit any other phase of life to the One who made us and redeemed us and invites us to cast on Him our every care. In fact, in turning over to Christ all that concerns him about sex, a Christian finds that he is not *robbed* of something pleasurable, but rather he is *given* something far richer and more

---

[3]Lester A. Kirkendall, *Premarital Intercourse and Interpersonal Relations* (New York: The Julian Press, Inc.), pp. 173-175.

wonderful and glorious than he has ever imagined![4] Sex, like everything else surrendered to Christ, takes on a new luster and purity and meaning.

Indeed, it is the one who fears that God will spoil the pleasure of sex if it is surrendered to Him who in the end will experience loss. Jesus said, "Anyone who wants to follow Me must put aside his own desires and conveniences and carry his cross with him everyday and *keep close to Me! Whoever insists on keeping his life will lose it, but whoever loses his life for My sake will save it*" (Luke 9:23, 24, *Living Gospels*).

---

[4]For a beautiful illustration of this truth, see C. S. Lewis's fantasy, *The Great Divorce* (New York: The Macmillan Company, 1946). In one scene, lust is personified as an ugly, whispering, wriggling lizzard attached to a man to torment and control him. The man is apprehensive about turning it over to God, because he learns that this would mean the creature must die. When at last in desperation the man permits the Angel of God to kill the lizard, he is startled to see not a lifeless corpse, but an amazing transformation taking place! The lizard which had so long held him in slavery is changed into a strong, handsome, silvery-white stallion on which the man — himself also transformed — rides off in triumph and richness of life.

Postscript

In attempting to set forth a Christian philosophy of sex and to answer the questions of many who are wondering about the Bible's teachings on premarital sex, there is always the danger that some readers will assume that, because of past conduct, the Biblical ideal has little to offer them. Thus, perhaps a further word is in order here.

It is tragic that many Christians have acted as though the "loss of virginity" in the unmarried — no matter how, when, or why it occurs — means that a line has been crossed that makes one forever "unchaste," "impure," "a fallen woman," "a lewd and unclean young man," "soiled," "a person of loose morals or easy virtue," a participant in "the scarlet sin." Because of this widespread attitude, scores of young people and adults have concluded that the church has nothing to say to them. If Christianity has only *one* message in regard to sexual intercourse (save it till marriage), what of the person who desires to follow Christ's way at some time *after* sex has been experienced? Is that person doomed to a life of remorse without relief, to feelings of guilt and estrangement from God and His people, to a marriage that can never hope to attain anything close to Christ's ideal — all because of a past stained "too deep" to be reached by the cleansing power of the Saviour? Of course not!

When a prostitute wept at the feet of Jesus, washing them with her tears and kisses, wiping them with her hair, anointing them with sweet-smelling ointment, a self-righteous re-

ligious leader was offended. He wondered if Jesus didn't
realize she was a woman of the streets; otherwise, surely
He would have quickly put a stop to such disgraceful behavior. Reading the man's thoughts, Jesus taught him an
important lesson on love and forgiveness. Jesus looked into
the woman's heart. He saw her faith, her love for the
Saviour, her desire to experience redemption — to be rescued
from her empty life. He didn't deny the fact of her sins
(which he said were many), but He forgave her and said
to her, "Your faith has saved you: go (enter) into peace —
in freedom from all the distresses that are experienced as
the result of sin" (Luke 7:50, *The Amplified Bible*). She
was cleansed, restored, made whole in the sight of God.
She was — despite her past — *pure.*

Similarly, we might think of Jesus' encounter with the
woman at the well (John 4), who had been married five
times and now lived with a sixth man out of wedlock.
Transformed by Christ, she became an effective witness for
Him immediately.

Another incident pointing out Christ's compassion for the
person straying from God's will in regard to sex is the account of the adulterous woman brought to Him in John
8:1-11. We know little about her and nothing at all about
her sexual partner. Was she a lonely wife seeking for comfort and understanding in a lover's arms? Was she a single
woman having an affair with a married man? Were they
both married to others, but seeking thrills and adventure in
an extramarital romance? Were they looking for relief from
an unhappy home life? Were they an unmarried couple
experimenting with sex relations? The Scriptures give no
reason to conclude that the woman was a harlot as is often
assumed. All we know is that the Pharisees caught her in
the very act of coitus with someone other than her husband,
and they brought her to Jesus to see if He would carry out
the sentence of the law.

Instead, Jesus brought the woman's accusers face to face
with their own consciences. Was there a single one of them

who could honestly say he had never tasted of the sin for which they condemned the woman — in fantasy or lustful gazing if not in actual act? Who would cast the first stone? The oldest men paused and reflected over many years, then walked away one by one. Even the youngest men could not deny their own sinful desires and practices.

Soon all were gone except Jesus and the woman. Jesus did not hesitate to call adultery *sin.* But He pronounced words of pardon and hope: " 'Woman, where are they? Has no one condemned you?' She said, 'No, one, Lord.' And Jesus said, 'Neither do I condemn you; go, and do not sin again' " (John 8:10-11). "For God sent not his Son into the world to condemn the world, but that the world through him might be saved. He that believeth on him is not condemned; but he that believeth not is condemned already, because he hath not believed in the name of the only begotten Son of God. . . . There is therefore now no condemnation to them which are in Christ Jesus . . ." (John 3:17, 18; Romans 8:1).

We must admire the honesty of the Pharisees in this instance. It must have been difficult for these proud, self-righteous men (who so often were guilty of hypocrisy) to walk away, thereby admitting that they, too, were sinners! Sad to say, there are no doubt some in the Christian church today who *would* have picked up that first stone and hurled it eagerly toward the one they judged a sexual transgressor, while closing their eyes to secrets locked in their own hearts and memories (as well as to all sorts of sins in realms other than the sexual). Some persons in Christian circles seem to fear that others may be led into sin if the Gospel is proclaimed as good news for those who have already tasted sexual experience. (It's strange that we don't hesitate to speak of Christ's forgiveness of the repentant thief out of fear that hearers will decide they're free to commit robbery because God will forgive them!)

However, let's not forget that vast numbers of the early Christians had participated in all kinds of sexual experiences before they were converted to Christ. The pagan religions out of which they were saved included cult prostitutes. Fornication and adultery were prevalent. Homosexual practices were widely engaged in. Men and women who had freely indulged in licentious living in their past life did not, because of this, feel they were less loved by God, less accepted by Christ, unworthy to be members of Christ's church. After all, wasn't this what the Gospel was all about — good news for the fallen, the burdened, the captive, the person who longed for freedom and wholeness and meaning and forgiveness? This isn't to deny the fact of sin and God's judgment upon it, of course, but to point out that Christ came to rescue us — to redeem us. Thus, St. Paul could list all sorts of practices (including sexual transgressions) characterizing those who "will not inherit the kingdom of God," but was able to add, *"And such were some of you"!* What made the difference? What brought about the change? "You were washed, you were sanctified, you were justified in the name of the Lord Jesus Christ and in the Spirit of God" (I Corinthians 6:9-11). Peter likewise had something to say to those in the Christian church who had lived sexually loose lives in the past but who had been transformed by Christ. (See I Peter 4:2-5.)

Thus, it is an insult to God and a failure to comprehend the gospel message to conclude that what happened one night in the back seat of a car or on a motel bed or in someone's home or apartment is somehow beyond the scope of God's grace and redemptive power.

There is a message here for the Christian, too. There are those who have already trusted Jesus Christ, and have known what it means to be born anew into His kingdom, who nevertheless may slip and stumble into sexual sin on some occasion. Such a person may suffer terrible pangs of guilt and shame and may find it extremely hard to forgive himself — let alone to believe that *God* can forgive him. God has something to say to this person, too: "I write you this, my children, so that you will not sin; but if anyone does sin, we have Jesus Christ, the righteous, who pleads for us with the Father. For Christ himself is the means by which our sins are forgiven, and not our sins only, but also the sins of all men. . . . If we confess our sins to God, we can trust him, for he does what is right — he will forgive us our sins and make us clean from all our wrongdoing" (I John 2:1, 2; 1:9, TEV).

In the Old Testament, we read of David, a man who knew and loved God (in fact, God called him "a man after his own heart"), but who nevertheless committed the sin of adultery and then tried to cover it up by murder (II Samuel 11:2—12:24). True, David's sin caused deep problems and suffering — not only for himself, but for others also, and it greatly grieved the Lord — but David knew there was mercy and forgiveness with God, and he gratefully accepted God's pardon. (See Psalm 51, written at this time. Also read Psalm 32.)

There isn't one of us who can boldly say with absolute certainty that never would it be possible for us to be sexually tempted or to succumb to such temptation. "So be careful. If you are thinking, 'Oh, I would never behave like that' — let this be a warning to you. For you too may fall into sin" (I Corinthians 10:12, *Living Letters*). There is no room for smugness here. Christians have no right to look down their noses upon a brother or sister Christian who has taken some missteps in regard to sex, or to shun an unbeliever who has never learned what it means to conform to God's standards of sexual conduct. "Brethren, if a man is overtaken in any trespass, you who are spiritual should restore him in a spirit of gentleness. Look to yourself, lest you too be tempted" (Galatians 6:1).

But there is hope. Immediately after the Apostle Paul warns the one who thinks he stands that he, too, might fall (and the context specifies sexual immorality among other things), he adds: "But remember this, the wrong desires that come into your life aren't new and different. Many others have faced exactly the same problems before you. And you can trust God to keep temptation from becoming so strong that you can't stand up against it, for He has promised this and will do what He says. He will show you how to escape temptation's power so that you can bear up patiently against it" (I Corinthians 10:13, *Living Letters*).

Christ offers His resources. It is up to us to trust Him and ask His help. God promises a way of escape in time of temptation. It is up to us to *choose* His way.

> But O my God! though grovelling I appear
> Upon the ground, and have a rooting here
> Which pulls me downward, yet in my desire
> To that which is above me I aspire:
> And all my best affections I profess
> To Him that is the Sun of Righteousness.
> Oh! keep the morning of His incarnation,
> The burning noontide of His bitter passion,
> The night of His descending, and the height
> Of His ascension — ever in my sight!
> That, imitating Him in what I may,
> I never follow an inferior way.
>
> — GEORGE WITHER, 1588-1667

Index